Damaged 2 Delivered

Joyce M. Hester

AKA Lady Joy

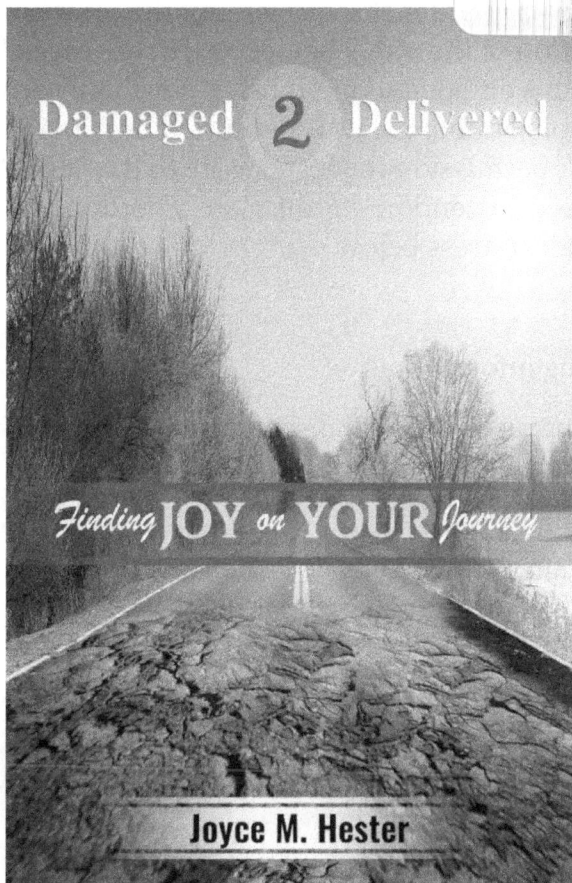

Copyright

Ordering information:

Quantity Sales - Special discounts are available for bulk purchases by corporations, associations, networking groups.

For details contact Lady Joy at iamtheladyjoy@gmail.com

ISBN 978-0-9991050-3-0

Table of Contents

Dedication

With a most gracious and thankful heart
I dedicate the writings in this book
to my heavenly Father.
Without Your grace, mercy, and most of all your love,
I wouldn't be here today.
In my life, you have always been Jehovah Elyon,
the Most High God, the one who is forever in control
of every situation and circumstance that concerns me.

In my times of loneliness, you have given me comfort.
When my tears were too much for me to bear,
you have wiped every tear from my eyes.
You, my Father, have never left me nor forsaken me
despite all the wrong I've done, and for that,
I will always and forever be thankful and grateful.
Writing this book has been difficult; however,
it's been therapeutic for me as well, and I'm thankful
that you trusted me to bring it to completion,
that you would get the glory out of every word shared.

Acknowledgements

To my sister by choice and my best friend in the whole world for life, Adrienne Quick, for always accepting me for who I am and loving me unconditionally. Through you, I have experienced what true friendship and unconditional love truly mean here on earth.

To my oldest and dearest friend, Heidi Hughey, for pouring the words "the opposite is true" into my spirit when things were mentally, emotionally and physically excruciating for me.

To all my Queen sisters, Pastor Cheryl Leak, Minister Sandra Strong, 1st Lady Kim Johnson, Marie Cleveland, Nia Fitzpatrick, Corliss White, Kim Williams, Donna Carlock, Julie Pounds, Pamela Mays, Vivian Desouza, Latisha Heath, Chi T Mathias, Michelle Kirkpatrick, LaMonique Fairbanks, Tanisha Moreland, Crystal Myers, Le'Laurelle and Judy Leonard. I am truly so blessed that there are too many to list them all here. They have prayed for me, encouraged me, allowed me to vent, and loved me to a fault, even when I was difficult to love. Know that there is not a day that passes that I don't think of each of you.

Last but never least, to my three beautiful children, the reasons why I have never given up: my oldest and only beautiful daughter Tashira, who is my dream; Nahshon, who is my prayer; and JoMaurie, who is my gift. I am thankful and grateful for the love I receive from each of you!

Foreword

We met at a conference in Savannah, Georgia.
However, we met way before then.

We were like kindred spirits, to which Joyce's spirit
hooked on to mine as she followed me into the
bathroom prior to me taking the stage to speak.

At first, I thought that was weird that this lady was
following me into the bathroom. She was so talkative,
too! I had to leave to go into the room to be ready to
speak and she wanted to have a meeting in the ladies'
room---I'm dating myself. That is a title of a song back
in the 70s, or 80s?

I am glad she listened to her inner self telling her to
talk to me. Here's why.

Fast forward about a year later, we reconnect as she
invited me to be on her radio show. I was honored.
We had a great time on the show. Prior to that, we had
a moment to talk and found out that our initiatives are
the same.

Joyce's book From Damage 2 Delivered is similar to
my book, Speak Your Voice.

We are both saying the same thing in our books. How
it is time to Speak Our Voices, Our Truths, Our
Crosses We Bore for the sake of someone's
Deliverance from Being Damaged.

From Damage 2 Delivered from the beginning to the
end challenges you to Speak Your Truth. To no longer
be in hiding of whatever trauma you have faced. This
book helps give yourself permission to get free from

your past and your pain and leverage it for not only your happiness, but simultaneously for others' happiness. Joyce paves the way and sets the tone for you to get free, get delivered and to get healed.

Know that your Voice Matters. Your Story Matters. Your Truth Matters and as Joyce would say "Your Joy Is Significant".

Joyce has helped countless others through her radio show and other means to triumph over their trials. She epitomizes resilience, strength, courage and wisdom, considering that she has been through such a horrific traumatic event and yet willing to selflessly unveil herself to you on what she went through and how she triumphed over her trial. I respect Joyce for that. Risking shame, ridicule, ostracism and all, Joyce is sharing her story with you in hopes you move from being Damaged to being Delivered.

Having counseled thousands as a Licensed Clinical Psychotherapist who have experienced mental health disorders for nearly 20 years, coached individuals as A Leadership and Life Coach through their trauma and pain to turn their pain into passion and profit, and spoken to countless others all over the world as a Award Winning Global Speaker to taking off limits to discover their next level of greatness and success, I have not met anyone taking massive action to transform lives and bring about significant breakthrough quite like Joyce Marie Hester. She is the Real Deal. She is a Big Deal. She is A One of A Kind.

May this book be the penicillin and peace for your pain. May Joyce's story move you to your breakthrough, healing, deliverance, transformation, and change. May you move from being damaged to being delivered. If you find it challenging to move forward alone, consider Joyce and her services in helping coach you through to your deliverance with her easy step by step From Damaged 2 Delivered process.

Make sure you inform everyone you know of this Breakthrough book. And pay it forward. Be selfless and purchase multiple copies of From Damaged 2 Delivered so that you can play part into others' breakthrough, too. This is your time. This is your moment. Take it.

Your Deliverance awaits.

Dr. Sarah Renee Langley
Author Speaker Coach
LeadHER International

Damaged: My Truth

Jeremiah 1:5 Before I formed you in the womb I knew you; before you were born I sanctified you; I ordained you as a prophet to the nations.

INNOCENCE-

This is the beautiful, ugly, transparent story of my life. God predetermined that I would write my journey over 42 years ago before I was even born. Before I was a dot in my mother's belly, God knew everything there was to know about me. He knew the good, the bad, the ugly, and the not--so-pretty parts of my life. God was also my rock when I experienced physical, emotional, and mental challenges.

I was born in Quincy, Florida – a little town outside of Tallahassee, Florida – to Lillie and Elbert Allen, and was raised in Fort Walton Beach, Florida. My mother was a domestic engineer (housewife to some) who was an amazing seamstress, cook, and hairstylist to not only her family, but to the community as well. There wasn't much, that I knew of anyway, that my mother couldn't do. She was a naturally creative person.

My father worked for Okaloosa County doing anything from janitorial work to working on the city roads. He was a very hard worker and provided for our family. My parents made sure that we were clothed, fed, and overall, they made sure we had the things we needed and some of the things we wanted.

I am child number five out of six children. I often thought of my family as the black Brady Bunch since we had a mom and dad with three boys and three girls. Except, there was no Alice the Maid. Nevertheless, the beautiful part of my family, for us kids anyway, was that we always had someone to play with.

We were a religious family and church was a second home and part of our routine. The entire family attended Wednesday night bible study, Friday night revivals, Sunday morning services and Sunday evening services. My siblings and I had Sunday school, too. There were also frequent week-long revivals often held during the summer months. I remember those revivals so vividly because the women on the motherboard would all have their hand-held paper fans in full motion. We spent all that time in church, supposedly serving God but we were literally living a home life filled with so much hell and full of the devil, especially from where I was standing. I'm sure from the outside looking in, we were a normal, seemingly happy family. Yet, we were far from the model church family or the Brady Bunch image that we projected.

We were so entrenched in the church that when we were sick as children, our mother would take us to the church. She would often tell me stories of a particular time I was sick with thrush at six months old. Thrush is a painful oral yeast infection that appears on the sides, roof, gums, tongue and lips of a baby's mouth. The thrush that I had was so severe, it spread out of my mouth, down my chin, under my neck and caused me to be sick near death. I had lost a dangerous amount of weight because it was painful for me to take a bottle. My mother did what the bible said and took me to the elders of the church. They prayed a prayer of healing over my tiny little body, and my mother believed that once they touched and agreed, I began to slowly heal, regained an appetite, got my weight back up, and ultimately my health back as well.

Later in my adolescent years, at age eleven to be exact, I developed diabetes and was hospitalized for a brief period of time. I had to learn how to take care of myself when I wasn't at home with my mother. Needless to say, managing diabetes as a child was extremely difficult.

My mom used to also recall my toddler days when I was a true daddy's girl. I can't fully remember that period of time, although I've always wished to have those positive images of our relationship in my mental database. He was the only one that could quiet me down when I'd cry as a baby. When I started walking, I would be the one to run after him as he was walking out the door to go work. I wish I could remember those times!

I do have my own good memories of my father. He had a sweet tooth and loved candy just as much as we did. I'm sure my mom did not like it, but he always has treats for us kids. I can still smell that old-school Brut fragrance he wore, and my dad had an amazing smile that I believe I inherited. My father also had a beautiful voice. As a deacon in our church he quite frequently sang with in quartet group with some other church men. He could sing! In retrospect, I truly admired so much about him. That's how it started out for me, but a life-altering event took place that would redirect my feelings toward my father for years to come.

Matthew 18:4-6 Therefore, whoever takes the lowly position of this child is the greatest in the kingdom of heaven. And whoever welcomes one such child in my name welcomes me. If anyone causes one of these little ones - those who believe in me - to stumble, it would be better for them to have a large millstone hung around their neck and to be drowned in the depths of the sea.

SHATTERING OF INNOCENCE-

I was seven years old and like most children that age, I loved cookies and other treats. My mother kept a large cookie jar on the kitchen counter filled with big vanilla crème cookies. Oh, how I loved those cookies! My siblings and I were always outside playing so when I thought no one was in the house, I would sneak a few of the cookies out of the jar and go enjoy them privately. On the day that changed my life, I snuck into the house to get some cookies. My mom and my sisters left the house for a walk. Just as I was putting the lid back on the jar with my three cookies in hand, I turned around to see my father was standing there. I got caught for the first-time stealing cookies from the cookie jar.

I thought for sure that I was about to get a whipping, but I didn't. What did happen next changed my life forever. I was about seven years old and I was scared out of my mind because he told me to come to him, but he didn't tell me to put the cookies back. I just knew for sure I was going to get a beating. Instead, he took me into the living room, turned the television on, sat me on the right side of his lap, and told me to go ahead and eat my cookies.

I was not ready for or expecting what took place next. In that moment he began caressing, hugging and gently feeling up and down on my thigh with his forefinger encouraging me to eat my cookies. I remember trying to eat those cookies, but it was awkward to say the least, because I knew right from wrong and taking those cookies was wrong. In my mind, I should have been getting punished for what I had done. At that moment, I was confused because I wasn't being punished for taking the cookies.

He pulled me closer to him. I remember having a little skirt on. Even though I was outside playing, it was against our belief as Church of God in Christ members for women and girls to wear shorts or pants. He was holding me with his right arm wrapped around me as if I were a little baby. He took his left hand and slowly rubbed his hand back and forth on my left thigh, as he slowly made his way up my skirt. I wasn't quite sure what was going on at the time, and I didn't know what to do. He then pulled my legs apart and put his big hand down my panties and he began touching my vaginal area while simultaneously telling me to eat my cookies and not to tell anybody. He said, "This is our little secret." Those secrets nearly destroyed me. Secrets ate me up on the inside and at times caused bouts of depression. They caused hurt, pain and disappointment. As a result, I now refuse to keep secrets.

Honestly, I don't think I had the words in my vocabulary to verbalize what was taking place at that time to anyone. Just as he was saying those words to me, one of my brothers came in from outside to get water. My father lifted me off his lap, sat me beside him and acted as if we were just watching the television. That was the first day that I never ate all of the cookies that I took out of the cookie jar. That was also the first time my father touched me inappropriately, or at least that's my first memory of him violating me. That first time he touched me I was left feeling confused, perplexed and not knowing what to do. As an adult I think back to that time as a seven-year-old little girl and I want to believe that I knew what had happened was wrong but didn't have the words or even experience to express it.

In my opinion, innocence is a childlike state that we are all born into where we know absolutely nothing. Innocence is the lack of experience and knowledge about the world and all the bad things that happen in it.

A child's innocence is beautiful because a child is allowed and expected to be imaginative. Innocence is believing that a chubby Santa Claus can fit down the skinny chimney. I believed Santa Claus Innocence is believing that the tooth fairy comes in the middle of the night while you are sleeping and leaves money under your pillow when you lose a tooth. Innocence is – and this is my favorite one – that there is really an oversized bunny that lays Cadbury chocolate eggs at Easter time.

Most adults enjoy the innocence of children. Watching the excitement of a young child leaving cookies for Santa Claus and waiting for presents is heartwarming and satisfying. Every child has a right to believe with their imagination until reality and maturity sets in.

Innocence can also be heartbreaking at the moment it is robbed from a child before the child has had the natural mind development to understand the realities of how awful life situations can truly be. It is also heartbreaking when a child is forced into the reality that there is so much evil in the world and they have become a part of the viciousness, or when the purity of a child is erased at the hands of those he or she trusts.

I believe it is a horrible thing to lead a child astray, then make the child go through intentionally inflicted damage by an adult who should know better. The pain and disappointment are devastating for the child. Because of my father, I was robbed of my innocence. He was supposed to protect me, provide for me and give me the tools to prosper.

Young children are not expected to go to work, pay the mortgage or rent, take care of the household expenses, cook the meals and do all of the shopping, yet here I was, exposed to adult behavior. I wasn't mature enough to stop it and had no real understanding of what I was to do. With every passing encounter, I slipped deeper into my feelings of low self-esteem, worthlessness, sadness, depression, pain, and very real disappointment.

I thought for a long time that what I was going through was what every little girl was experiencing. I did not want my father to molest me, but I think I just accepted what was happening. I loved him the most but he left me with a lasting pain that stuck with me for years into my adulthood. I was damaged when I should have been experiencing joy.

As time went by, the act of the violation became more frequent. I'm not certain as to why, but I was the only child in my family at that time that had their own room. I think it had to with my age, and I was a girl. My older sisters had a room together and the three boys all shared a room. I remember when my father started coming into my room at night. I would be awakened by him pulling the covers off of me, calling me by my childhood nickname (they called me "monk," my mom says because I was always swinging from something when I was little), followed by him touching my leg then my thighs and then always pulling my legs apart to get to my vaginal area.

I would pretend to be asleep, hoping that he would eventually get discouraged and stop, but that seemed to arouse him even more because it never stopped him. As an adult, even now as I write this book, I find myself not fully understanding how someone could bring such hurt to someone that loves them so much – someone they are supposed to love and protect.

By the time I was eleven, it seemed as if the frequency of the sexual abuse increased. During that time my father began to get bolder with his interaction towards me. I remember standing in the kitchen at the sink washing dishes and he would come behind me and pop me on my butt as if we were some kind of couple. He would always give me that it's our secret (which by this time was just understood; no words had to be spoken) with a smile on his face that always looked like the cat that ate the canary. I absolutely hated my dad for what he was doing to me and how what he was doing made me feel about myself, others, and ultimately the world at large.

I can remember very vividly the day that it became clear to me that what my father had been doing to me was wrong. It was during third grade. One day, the school called all the students to the cafeteria for a puppet presentation on "good touch, bad touch." The moment came, there in that lunch room, when the light of revelation came on for me. As we were all sitting there, what I already kind of felt was wrong was confirmed – what was going on in my home between my father and me was not supposed to be happening.

As I was sitting there in shock, I happened to look to the right of me and one of my classmates (we will call her Ashley) was crying uncontrollably. As soon as the teachers noticed Ashley crying, she was removed from the cafeteria that day and she never returned to the cafeteria or the school again.

I was filled with emotions just like Ashley was, but no tears were coming from my eyes. However, I immediately became angry, scared and confused. I did not know what to do. I believe, even at eight years of age, that I was experiencing some kind of shock. I was overwhelmed with feelings of guilt, disgust, pain, and shame. From that day forward, I was in a state of worry because I didn't know who to trust or tell.

I couldn't stop thinking about Ashley. As a child, I assumed that what was happening to me was also happening to her. My already looming fear deepened now with the thought that *if I tell, I might disappear, too*. I was literally frozen with fear. As a child, you just don't know what to do, and because of that not knowing, for me it allowed this abuse to progress and continue for five more years.

I watched the one who was supposed to care for, love, and protect me act as if everything was okay and normal. We still attended church several times a week. I played with the neighborhood kids, visited relatives, and went to school like nothing was happening. But almost everything in my home life at that time was, for me, a big, ugly lie that I was forced to live.

I was fortunate enough to have a third-grade teacher, Mrs. Dukes, that I loved. I still remember her gentle face to this very day. I want to believe that she somehow sensed that something was wrong with me. Mrs. Dukes treated me very kindly and I became known as the teacher's pet. Her classroom provided a secure, peaceful place where I was respected and she gave me the opportunity to be close to her.

Although the molestation continued and all I wanted to be was invisible, Mrs. Dukes made me feel like it was okay to be visible. She always called on me to assist her. She liked me and I looked forward to going to her class every day. For the duration of that third-grade year, being her student assistant was the one thing that truly made me feel okay, and that was important for me. Unfortunately, for me it still wasn't enough for me to trust her and share with her the horrible things that were happening to me at home. That allowed the molestation to continue.

My father convinced me that what was happening between him and me was our secret, and he was always giving me candy and quarters. He always had treats for us kids and we loved it, but I grew to hate his sweet tooth because he used candy as some sort of pass for the wrong that he was doing. After every act of abuse, he would give me me dollars or quarters and candy.

I didn't know that what was happening to me was wrong until that play where we learned about "bad touch" in school. Over the years, I have thought about what happened to my classmate. I can only assume that she, too, was going through the same inexcusable conditions at her home, and finally child protective services stepped in and began protecting her.

It's not right that any child should have to experience any abuse, sexual or otherwise, especially from a close family member – someone she/he loves, trusts, and would do anything to make happy. When the light was finally turned on for me, even though I endured those repeated encounters for several more years, I now knew that it was wrong and that I wasn't to blame.

As I reflect back to my early childhood years, I'm sure that all I wanted was to be loved, respected, and most of all protected. Childhood moments are supposed to be times of innocence, free of worries, fun-filled, and imaginative. Our minds are fragile during those times in our lives. We shouldn't be exposed to the cruel world before a level of understanding has been established. However, for me all of that was shattered, all of that was destroyed. All of that was damaged by the one I should have been able to look at as a hero and protector, the one who was supposed to scare all the boys off, the one who I loved like a little girl should. The one I called daddy.

At first, because I had so much love in my heart for my father and no real understanding, I didn't know that what was happening between him and me was wrong. Because of that, I wanted to keep this secret, his secret. Keeping it for so long caused a lot of things in my life to spiral out of control.

By the time I was in the fourth grade, my grades went from excellent to poor. I now believe that because of what was happening at home, I really couldn't focus like I should have. I brought home a really bad report card and reluctantly gave it to my mother. If my memory serves me correctly, I had all F's and a D on that particular report card. My mother sent me to my room and I was told to stay there until my father got home from work. When he got there, he took me into the bathroom, had me lie on the floor, straddled me, and beat the crap out of me.

I tell that story (1) because I need you, as you read this book, to see the damage that took place early on in my life; (2) so that you can see as well how the abuse affected me as far as my focus and keeping up with my school work. I never deserved that cruel beating for getting those bad grades because of what he was doing to me. To be beaten on top of the sexual abuse, how could I be anything other than damaged?

During that beating, I don't remember crying at all, but I was very enraged. While putting my thoughts and memories into this book, I have been able to release those tears for the little girl Joyce who lives on the inside of me, so that she can move forward and truly walk as an adult in the essence of her God-given name, "Joy."

The molestation stopped when I was 13. By this time, I had developed a serious attitude. I was angry about what was happening to me and all the lies that went with it. I had made up in my mind that I was going to make him leave me alone. We had a laundry room off of our kitchen and there was a pantry door next to that where snacks and non-perishable items were kept. I was going to the pantry one day and my father came behind me and touched my arm to get my attention. I looked him dead in his eyes and despite all of the anger, fear and frustration I was holding onto, a boldness came over me and I told him to never touch me again. From that day forward, he never touched me again.

JUSTICE DENIED-

Ecclesiastes 3:17 I said in mine heart, God shall judge the righteous and the wicked: for there is a time there for every purpose and for every work.

In September of 1989, I turned fifteen years old. One warm afternoon, I was standing in my front yard near the curb of the street with a group of the neighborhood kids just cooling. I talked and laughed with my friends but inside my emotions swirled out of control. It was more than teenage angst; I knew that what my father had done to me was wrong. I knew my promiscuity was not the correct way to live. But I didn't know how to express myself or how to right the wrongs. I didn't know how to feel better.

My friends did not know what was creeping inside me, just below surface. We sat around on that lazy day not really knowing what the other person was feeling or going through. Suddenly, as if a sign from God, one of our friends came running down the street towards us yelling that a good friend of ours, Tracy, had tried to kill herself. I began to scream *"WHY?"* several times. Apparently, my friends knew what was happening to Tracy but I simply did not know. My friend tells me that Tracy's father had been molesting her for quite a while and she couldn't take it anymore and attempted to take her life.

I felt moved at hearing about Tracy. She and I were bonded. She understood the pain and shame. I didn't want to kill myself. I wanted to feel free right then and out in the open. I began screaming, "Me too! Me too!" I had only admitted the abuse to one other person, my then-boyfriend, before that time. My mother was standing nearby and overheard what had been said by me and my friend and my mother called for me to come to her. I was emotionally charged, frightened, astonished as I walked towards her. I walked toward my mother feeling frightened. As I got closer, I heard, "Not my baby!" which is what most mothers' reaction should and would have been expected to be.

I felt a sense of relief that my mom was ready and waiting to comfort me. But by the time I reached her, the words coming out of her mouth had quickly become venomous. She began spewing nasty and angry words toward me. The woman who was supposed to protect and love me was calling me names! "You slut! You whore!" Those words felt like knives cutting away my flesh. She was literally blaming me for the molestation!

My mother went into the house to confront my father and an argument ensued wherein my father denied he had ever touched me. In either desperation, shame, or some cunning ploy to get my mother not to leave him, my father grabbed a shotgun from the closet, got on his knees, and threatened to kill himself. I watched him get on his knees with my mother distraught, not because he had molested me, but because he had been weak enough to touch me. It was as if I had tempted him and he couldn't resist.

Confusion set in and I felt my head pounding with first rage, then hurt, and finally shame. It seemed to overtake me like those outer body experiences people always talk about in the movies. Except, this was not fiction. I was real and what he did to me was *real* and *disgusting*. I waited for him to pull the trigger so that he could pay. Maybe I could go back to being the little girl who was mischievous and playful. Maybe the shame would go away. Maybe I could get my innocence back.

Seconds passed as I waited for my justice. "Just do it!" I thought. It did not take long for me to realize that my father was not going to pull the trigger on that shotgun. So, with a determination I never knew I had, I demanded, "Give me the gun. I will blow your head off for you!"

My mother looked me in the eyes and saw the impending doom. She pleaded, "Don't give it to her!" She knew I was definitely more serious about killing him than he was about killing himself. I thought, "Let me end this for both us." My father refused to give me the gun. Instead he stood up on his feet and walked away and my mom followed him. I stood there still in a state of shock. I went to my room, holding my pregnant belly and cried myself to sleep.

The next day my father moved out for a short time and the weight of guilt fell on me. I was the reason he left. Still, he moved back in and my mother remained married to my father. We all stayed in the same home. Things did change though. A silence blanketed our house and that silence continues to this day. For a period of time it seemed as if I were the outcast in the family. No one really said much to me, which made me feel even worse about myself. It was as if I had done some awful thing to my entire family by exposing this nasty not so little secret. Even till this very day I stand alone in the effort to uncover the long-standing secret that not only happened in my home but many other homes around the world. My mother whom I love with all my heart our relationship has suffered over the years as I gained the confidence and the strength to truly find my voice and began to speak out about this. Currently we seldom talk. My two sisters and I don't speak at all. My three brothers and I speak when I reach out to them. Otherwise we don't speak. It is sad but unfortunately it is my reality. I can only hope and pray that we can find some sort of restoration before it is too late.

That was an extremely hard time for me. It was truly damaging to realize how I saw, thought, and felt about myself, as well as my perspective on life that was forever changed. Today, I am thankful that I didn't have that opportunity to take his life. But I didn't always feel that way.

Despite a lot of effort on my part to understand it from my mother's perspective, I never could comprehend how my mother chose to stay with my father after learning the truth about what he had done. I did, however, resolve within myself that it was my mother's decision. I didn't allow it to affect the love I had for my mother.

Perhaps Tracy had more support at home than I did. I'm told by a mutual friend that she received the help she needed after attempting suicide. She is now living a full and productive life. We never got the chance to talk about what we both were experiencing and how it affected us. However, I'm glad that we both survived that day.

A MOTHER NOT READY

Psalm 127:3 Behold, children are a heritage from the Lord, the fruit of the womb a reward. KJV

My father's abuse lead me down some short roads of promiscuous behavior. *Research from the National Center for PTSD states that sexual abuse victims suffer from PTSD as adults, sexual promiscuity, prostitution, depression and trust issues.* The effects of child sexual abuse can be a lifelong and affect the victim's mental state in unimaginable ways. Of course, I did not understand that I was a victim who needed help. I did not know that my father had forced me to think that sex was equated with getting something. He gave me treats when he wanted to touch me. That's all I knew.

At 13, I looked older than I was, so I was able to get into clubs and hang out with the older crowd. Once I realized the power that I had as a female, I used that power for my own personal benefit. I believed that all men wanted from women was sex, so I knew that I could have any man I wanted at any given time. I used men like men used women. If I wanted to sleep with you, I would, and it was just for that time. I wasn't looking for you to be my man.

I became the great pretender. Since I didn't trust Mrs. Dukes enough to tell her what was going on in my home, I was continually being abused by a father that I loved. That love turned to hate for a long time and resulted in me losing out on many of my childhood years and left me in a web of confusion for many of my adult years.

From childhood to adulthood, I overcompensated for my father exploiting my trust by becoming a people-person in order to hide the shame and embarrassment of doing what a girl should never be called upon to do.

I became sexually active with more than one partner at age 13 and pregnant at age 15. I was actually pregnant at the time I revealed to my friends and mother that I had been molested by my father. I didn't care about much in life at that time except for always finding ways to be rebellious, smart-mouthed, sassy, and always sexy. I was fueled with a lot of anger and would lash out for any reason, big or small. My emotions would boil over and spill out onto my neighborhood street a couple of years later, but until then, I sought refuge in others. Looking for acceptance, respect, and ultimately love, I jumped into a relationship that I wasn't mentally ready for at all.

I became pregnant by a young man that would later become my husband. Being pregnant and becoming a mom at sixteen was very hard physically because of the diabetes, mentally because I was still stuck in a mindset that had not fully matured properly, and emotionally because I was full of fear, excitement and sheer confusion about who and what I was to be.

At the beginning of my pregnancy I had the support of my circle of friends. By the time I was eight months pregnant, however, my circle of friends had gotten considerably smaller. I'm sure that I wasn't deemed the best influence by my friends' parents. I felt alone a lot of the time during my pregnancy, so I found myself often talking to the little life that was growing on the inside of me.

I loved my baby so much before I ever delivered her, and I made a vow to myself to protect her and make her life better than mine had been. I had my daughter at sixteen and she became my reason to want to be a better individual. This wouldn't happen overnight, but I have always been one to never stop when I make my mind up, no matter what.

As a teenage mom, I found myself becoming extremely overprotective of my daughter almost immediately. I didn't want what happened to me to happen to her, so I over parented. I overcompensated. I made sure she was never alone; she was never in a position where she could be taken advantage of or ever feel like she wasn't protected by me as her mother. I even unconsciously placed a wedge between my daughter and her father.

I was the primary parent because he was gone with the military a lot of the time. I could not bear the thought of something like what happened to me happening to her. My parenting was laser focused on making sure that she never became me. I talked a lot to my daughter about everything. I know now that some of this was too much for her, but at the time I thought I was arming her with the knowledge she would need to protect herself in the event that I couldn't be with her.

I wanted to make sure she was well-informed about the things that I didn't know growing up, so I chose to share with her raw details about the perversion that existed in the world both near and far. I was trying to prevent her from ever experiencing any of the hurt, trauma, sorrow, and ultimately the damage that I had experienced as a child. I subconsciously made her my best friend, which fogged the mother-daughter relationship tremendously.

In the process of what I thought was excellent parenting and protection, I didn't realize I was keeping my daughter from becoming who God wanted her to be. I was literally smothering her. I found out the hard way that there is a thin line between protecting someone and controlling someone.

I was definitely controlling every move she made. I was a permanent fixture in her school career. I chaperoned everything, and I mean everything!!! I would even fight other children for my daughter. What mature mother or father does that? I promise I'm not exaggerating. She will tell you her mom was "team too much." This was all a direct result of the damage that I experienced as a child, and not ever dealing with it before becoming a mother or a wife.

My goal was to keep my daughter's environment positive and keep her from going through any hurt, but I ended up causing her some of the pain that I was trying so desperately to keep her from. We went through some very troubling times. We were good up until about her senior year of high school and her freshman year of college. That's when I knew she was tired of my hovering; however, I know now that she was done way before that time. When I finally realized it, it was way too late to make amends – at that time anyway.

I truly thought that I was the cool mom, and most of her friends did too, until I started getting involved in their teenage squabbles. I told you I was trying to keep

all pain away from my daughter, so much so that if I would hear about one of her friends doing her wrong or saying something that hurt her feelings, I would go into "mommy to the rescue" mode and confront that friend. I was *that* mom, just crazed with the idea that I had to protect her at all times.

Looking back at her preteen to teenage years, I realize that a lot of what I did for my daughter wasn't all bad, but it was far from all good. All this happened because of the abuse that took place all those years before, and I had no balance. You couldn't have told me then, but I know now that I was out of control and all over the place.

Bear in mind that I also have two boys that I was just as protective of, but I was able to ease up on them because they were "boys" and I thought they could protect themselves after the age of thirteen. Thank God, my daughter and I survived. We truly recovered. I'm very grateful to God that today she and I have a healthy, free, true mother-daughter relationship.

Psalm 50:15 And call upon me in the day of trouble: I will deliver thee, and thou shalt glorify me. KJV

It Won't Wash Away

After the molestation stopped, I had so many feelings that I had to work through and honestly, I didn't know where to begin. I felt emotional numbness, guilt, self-blame, loss of confidence, mood changes, low self-esteem, and for me the worst feeling of all was that feeling of dirtiness. For a long time, I always felt dirty and I began compulsively washing myself several times a day.

I would literally jump into a shower three, sometimes four times a day trying to physically wash away all of the ugly feelings that had been living in my brain for all those years. Honestly during this time, I would feel good after every one of those showers, but it was only for a short a while. Soon the feelings would resurface all over again. I was in a perpetual state of being, and the effects of being stuck in that place worsened with every wash.

To say that I rubbed my skin till it was red would be an understatement. I saw myself as dirty, nasty even. Unless you have been through any type of sexual abuse or trauma, you may have a hard time understanding what I am referring to about the feelings of being unclean. It's a flood of uncontrolled emotions that you go through. The unclean feeling that I was experiencing sometimes turned into rage, which was why I would rub my skin raw. I was angry, and I was taking the anger out on myself.

I would definitely say that I was going through feelings of hostility, anger, and depression. In my mind, I thought if I took enough showers I would eventually wash it all away. They had to be showers, because if I took a bath, my thought was always that I was sitting in the filth that I scrubbed off, and I would still have to run a shower.

For me, and I'm sure for many others who have survived child sexual molestation, the effects of the actions I was subjected to lasted many years after the abuse had ended. PLEASE KNOW THAT THERE IS NO TIMELINE FOR DEALING WITH AND RECOVERING FROM THIS KIND OF EXPERIENCE.

After about three to five years of trying to wash away the feelings that had been embedded in me for what seemed my whole life, I had to get some help. For the first time I began to really cry out to God. God strategically placed me in churches where the man and woman of God took me into their inner circles and truly treated me like their daughter; they accepted me into their family.

I remember my family and I were stationed in upstate NY and we were visiting a church for the first time as guests of some friends of ours. The pastor of the church was preaching, and he stopped his sermon and called my then-husband and I to the front of the church. He took his microphone away from his mouth and began to speak a word that I knew could have only come from God, because at that time in my life I wasn't talking about anything that happened in my childhood to anyone.

That pastor knew details about me that only God knew, and he took me by the hand and walked me through a year of counseling, which for me was the beginning of my deliverance. It also helped me see that there was no way I could wash away all the feelings inside of me, but God could. I won't tell you that through that process I was healed or delivered completely. I will tell you, though, that it gave me JOY to know that I was on God's mind and that He saw me and what I was going through.

I was able to ease up on scrubbing myself raw in the showers. Over the next few years, I went from three to four showers a day to what I hope is normal for everyone – one to two showers a day.

Other pastoral relationships that I am sure were by God's design came after the experience with the New York pastor. I felt like God wanted me to know the trust and the protection of a father. The pastors that God allowed me to cross paths with were spiritual fathers for me, and those experiences were nice. They were men of God who didn't want anything physically from me; they really only wanted me to be free from all of the hurt that my biological father had caused. I will forever be grateful for my time with those pastors, their wives, children, and the church families, because every encounter helped me to move forward a little bit more.

DELIVERED

Free to Be Me

Psalm 118:5 Out of my distress I called on the Lord; the Lord answered and set me free. ESV

There is a quote by author Rachel Wolchin that I love: "Before the truth can set you free, you need to recognize which lie is holding you hostage." I was that one who believed all the negative things that came at me. I'm not just talking about things I heard people say to me or the names that I was called. I'm also referring to the things that even the enemy whispered in my ears. I took those things and magnified them in my own life.

I want you to see that often the "enemy" is "in-a-me." We can be our own worst enemy. You see, I couldn't see anything that was positive about me as a person, or how I could be a positive influence in anyone's life because of how my own life was. I believe that the enemy attacks many of us in our minds when we are young, defenseless, and have no reasoning of how to combat negative things with positive ones, and we end up just believing the negative things for way too long.

There were so many negative words that I allowed to be repeated in my thought process over the years. Things like "you are dumb," "you're ugly," "you aren't smart enough," "ain't nobody trying to listen to you," "no one likes or wants you," "you're a whore," "you're a slut," "you're a four-eyed fool," "you look like a jack-o-lantern" – and this is just my short list. I didn't know how to silence those words...not by myself at least. I allowed these words to keep me in states of bondage for much of my life with feelings of worthlessness.

I'll say this: whoever said "sticks and stones may break your bones, but words will never hurt you" had it all backward from my perspective. Words *do* hurt and, in my case, they almost killed me.

When I was about eleven years old, I had this major crush on the older brother of one of my really good friends. I can remember almost drooling every time I had the opportunity to be around him. He was SO FINE, HANDSOME, AND JUST HOT! Yes, I was crushing hard and I would do anything to sit, stand, or just walk past him. I remember thinking how he had the smoothest, creamiest looking skin, just beautiful I tell you!

My friend would have sleepovers at her house from time to time. I remember there were a lot of us there for her birthday slumber party and we were all playing some childhood game, and my friend's brother called me "his little jack-o-lantern" -- it seemed like it was just blurted out. I was completely crushed! I don't even think he meant for it to hurt my feelings the way that it did. That phrase, "my little jack-o-lantern," haunted me for a long time.

First of all, as a child I always disliked certain things that represented Halloween, like witches, ghosts, black cats, and jack-o-lanterns. I thought jack-o-lanterns were scary and really ugly. When my friend's brother called me his little jack-o-lantern because of the gap in my top teeth, from that day forward I was self-conscious about my smile. I didn't want to ever smile again. If I did smile, I was so self-conscious about the space between my teeth, I would cover my smile. I wanted braces so badly. For much of my life, I often thought every person who saw my smile thought I looked like a jack-o-lantern. When I did manage to smile, most of the time I would smile not showing my teeth. That was when I was 11; I'm 42 today and I now smile without concern about that phrase "jack-o-lantern" that I internalized thirty-one years ago.

I share that story to show how words that are negatively spoken or that we perceive as negative can be powerful and keep us paralyzed and unable to move forward in our purpose as God intends for us all to do. For years, I let those words hold me hostage, unable to share what I now know is an amazing smile. I receive compliments all the time about my smile because I have stopped believing the lie that the enemy tried to keep me believing for all those years that my smile was ugly like an ugly jack-o-lantern. I now walk in the truth that God created in me this smile, to smile often and impact those that cross my path with positivity, cheerfulness, and JOY.

We ultimately create our own reality from what we choose to believe about ourselves through intention or inattention. If we don't consciously choose our beliefs about ourselves, we unconsciously absorb beliefs from our surroundings – beliefs that nine times out of ten are just not the truth. The truth, the way I see it, is that the better love, understand, and appreciate ourselves, the better we love, understand, and appreciate the world.

We are free to believe what we want, and I now choose to believe that I am the head and not the tail, above only and never beneath. I am a leader and not a follower, and I am the apple of God's eye. I believe that.

My life has been one that was broken. I had to realize that brokenness was only a temporary state of being and not a place of permanence. I had to realize that I could move from that broken place. I could be put back together again. Although I was shattered into many pieces, that shattering has led me to a place of being a product of all those fragmented pieces, which is a culmination of the beautiful person God made me to be.

As a grown woman, looking back on the years that I went through the molestation, I realized that my identity was stolen from me as a child and I carried those feelings of not knowing who I was through to the day I turned forty because I did not like what I saw in myself. The things that happened to me as a child caused a significant identity crisis in me and caused me to want to be everything for everyone that had a place in my life.

Our identity is the way we define ourselves starting in those preteen through adolescent years. Those years were hard for me. Was I a little girl or was I supposed to step into a womanly role before my time? Was I supposed to be playing with dolls or sitting on a man's lap pleasing him? Lots of questions about who I was played over and over in my head all the time, and sadly I just didn't know. I went through this war of identity crisis for what seemed to be forever.

What ultimately got me through the identity crisis was my realization of who God created me to be before I was in my mother's womb. To have a solid identity, we need to see that we are the same person in our past as we are in our present and will be in our future. I was always JOY!

This past year I started calling myself Lady JOY. I called my mother and told her that I was going by JOY now. She told me that when she was having me she was going to name me Joy but everyone around her encouraged her to name me Joyce, and so she did. It was really amazing for me to hear her tell me that, because it let me know that I was always destined to be JOY!

A person without a sense of identity can feel disconnected from who they are created to be, who they are or who they are to become. One day I looked in the mirror and asked myself, "Who am I?" I was finding it hard to believe that what I saw in my reflection was me. Think of someone getting into a terrible accident and their face being damaged or disfigured beyond recognition. Picture that person looking at their reflection utterly shocked by what is looking back at them, unable to believe what has happened to them. That is how I felt looking in the mirror, like I couldn't recognize what was looking back at me.

I thought my husband would provide me an identity. I thought he would provide me the answer to who I was. I was so wrong! While we experienced good and bad times together, there was still so much hurt that was unresolved in me. He had some controlling issues and I allowed things in the marriage that reflected what I had grown up with. Those feelings of not being protected resurfaced within my marriage. I allowed myself to be controlled, literally going from one identity crisis to the next. Not knowing who you are, not being able to identify with who God called you to be, will keep you in a posture of always making emotional decisions – decisions that will have you bound for years until you come to a place of knowing the true call on your life.

I choose to be JOY! JOY is not to be kept locked up inside of you imprisoned by your problems, circumstances, dramas, and traumas of your life. Those are the times when JOY should make its way to the surface of you. JOY is to be released, shared, and invoked into the world at large. JOY is having the freedom to fail and finally find the freedom to win.

In my own strength and efforts, trying to always figure out what to do next was exhausting at times, and I knew deep down inside that if it were not for God having His hand on me I would have been dead long ago. It is in that knowing that I realized God had a plan for my life. At birth, I was named Joyce, and that name embodies the concept of "JOY."

I am naturally a joyful, joyous person and I know that has been why the enemy has fought relentlessly to destroy me physically, spiritually, and mentally. When I tell you that I have been through more in my forty-three years of living then most people will see in an entire lifetime, that is not an exaggeration. Through child molestation, battling sickness and disease at an early age, self-esteem issues, holding on to bitterness as if it were some kind of badge of honor, and going through a divorce, I have had to dig down deep inside of myself to pull out enough strength to make it from day to day. Going from one trauma or drama to the next has been for me at times almost unbearable.

Nehemiah 8:10 speaks about the JOY of the Lord being your strength. You will find that Nehemiah, Ezra, and other leaders spent time reading the word of God to the people. As they read, the people began to weep in repentance, for they realized how badly they had failed the Lord. Nehemiah and the other leaders encouraged them to enjoy the feast, *for the JOY of the Lord is your strength.* I believe that they wanted the people to experience that JOY despite the wrong they had done. Nehemiah wanted them to realize that there was no benefit in falling into mourning and sadness.

The JOY of the Lord is what's inside of our hearts, and that JOY is the natural result of faith. It's a God-given gladness that comes through, I believe, consistent communication with God and getting to know Him more daily despite what we find ourselves going through. It is the gift, privilege, and result of that communication that I believe is His JOY – a JOY that only He can give and no one, I MEAN NO ONE, can take it away! That JOY that only God can give is why I have continued to survive, thrive, and live despite everything that was designed to destroy me from the time I was a baby until now. Your JOY may be lost, like mine was, but I stand as a witness that you, too, can find JOY on your journey. It is never too late!

As I journey through life, the only strength that I have had, the strength that has allowed me to be an overcomer, to obtain the blessings and victories, has been from God and God alone. There is a process called "introspection" which means looking within. Once I took that long, hard look at myself and saw that everything that I was trying in an effort to fix myself – to put myself back together again – just wasn't working, I cried out to God and I surrendered all to Him. I waved my white flag and said, "God, I can't do this without you."

He already knew that. I was the one who had to realize that He is the Most High God, the one who is in control of every situation and circumstance known and unknown in my life. He gets the glory for every victory in the story of my life. He is Jehovah Jireh, the one who has been my provider. God is both my source and resource. He is all that you or I truly ever need. Everything you or I need or want will fall into place as long as we keep God at the head of our lives.

I want to share how my painful experiences have allowed me to rise to a victory that I didn't even think possible. A victory of peace, love, and JOY that once you've heard my story will cause you to become introspective about your own life, and at the same time realize that success can come from struggle; there is a destiny for your disappointment and a purpose for your pain.

My introspection caused me to look long and hard at myself and helped me get to the other side of "through." My "through" was that I was through with my life, family, and friends. I wanted to be done with everything because I couldn't see the purpose for my being. I definitely battled with the thoughts of suicide, but I was raised in the church and I knew what killing myself meant, and that scared me more than my disillusionment and not wanting to live this life anymore. A state of confusion really set in. For all my sanctified folks, you know that where confusion is, the enemy is lurking.

Truly my life story has been directed by God. I believe that God sends people to be in your life and to be a part of your life for seasons, reasons, or lifetimes. I know without a doubt when it's all said and done that my life has been about God getting the glory. I've journeyed from trauma to drama, from *Damaged to Delivered*. As I look back over all the years I have been blessed to make it through, I can truly say that I have only seen one set of footprints in the sand. I know that it could have only been God carrying me through all the hurt, pain, sickness, the different diagnoses, the loneliness, disappointment, guilt, and shame. Without Him, I don't know where I would be, so I am forever grateful for His presence always in my life.

God Said I Am Beautifully and Wonderfully Made!

Psalms 139:14 I will give thanks and praise to You, for I am fearfully and wonderfully made; Wonderful are Your works; and my soul knows it very well.

There has to be a point in your life where you come into your natural, authentic self and just be the real you. *JOYFUL people don't have the best of everything, they make the best of everything.*

I had to learn to love myself first. But the layers of disappointment, mistrust, and the layers upon layers of frustration can make it impossible to even like yourself, much less love yourself. I had to come to a point where I found it okay to love myself. And that love only comes from being driven by God's love.

I recall looking at myself in the mirror, not seeing my worth, and literally hating what I saw. I hated everything about me – my hair, my skin, my lips, I hated my body. I couldn't see what God saw, and while having this private pity party as I stood looking in that mirror, I heard the voice of the Lord speak to my spirit. He told me how from the top of my head to the soles of my feet, I was made in His image, that I was FEARFULLY AND WONDERFULLY MADE, that He makes no mistakes, and that there were no mistakes in me.

He spoke, and I heard Him say that He placed every strand of hair on the top of my head, that the details of my face were His handiwork, that my eyes, nose, cheeks, chin, lips and teeth were designed by Him on purpose and with a purpose. Every scar that I have on my body, God allowed so that He could get the glory out of my life. Everything in me that I thought was broken and of no use, God told me was by His design. And with a loud audible voice, the Lord said to me, *"Daughter, you are beautiful because THAT is the way I made YOU!"* There's nothing like the love of God to tell you that you're not only beautiful but that you're valuable and that you have a purpose. That was the moment I knew that I was indeed a Queen.

1 Peter 2:9 But you are a chosen people, a royal priesthood, a holy nation, God's special possession, that you may declare the praises of him who called you out of darkness into His wonderful light.

Before I truly accepted or realized it, God had an assignment and a plan for my life, for me to share with as many young ladies as possible that they are not only beautiful, but that they are valuable, and that God has a purpose and a plan for their lives.

All too often, we can look back at the shame that we faced and the embarrassment that we've endured and say that we can't be used by God. That is the biggest trick that the enemy has. He wants to nail you to your past, confuse your present, and destroy your future. The hope of the enemy is that you would become stagnant and not bear fruit. We were created and saved by God to bear fruit. See John 15:3-8.

I need you to understand that the enemy wants us to be and remain unfruitful. To help you better understand unfruitfulness, take a look at the Parable of the Sower in Matthew 13:18-23. What I would like for you to understand is that after the three scenarios in this passage of scripture, the negative responses to Jesus' preaching, in the fourth scenario the seed is sown on good soil (verse 23).

The seed and soil represent those who hear and understand the word. Their hearts, the core of their very being, embrace the good news. They fight off the devil. They endure struggles and persecutions. They are not defined by worldly cares and wealth. They join the community that is committed to God's empire and are recognized by doing God's will. They live fruitful lives, signified by the abundant crop. So, like the parable, we have to position our own lives to succeed in a way that brings glory to the Kingdom of God. This takes daily action in cases like mine, where there was deep pain attached.

I said earlier that I only saw one set of footprints in the sand. I have often wondered, as I looked back on my life, who was walking with me? Who was there for me? Many people see the footprints of family, the footprints of friends, or the footprints of the whole village leading them to success in life. I only saw the footprints of God, but I often wondered why at times I felt so alone. I know now that those moments when I felt alone were the times that God was doing surgery on my heart, mind, body, and soul.

God pulled the curtain back and showed me that, yes, it was Him carrying me through the pain, hurt, disappointment, and all of the shame. He was also carrying me through the problems I found myself in, lifting me above the shame and transitioning me to a new name, a new place, and a new victory. That is what going from Damage to Deliverance is all about.

On that dreadful day that I heard my childhood friend tried to kill herself because of her secret pain, I was sure that she was battling feelings of worthlessness and shame. I believe she wanted to end her life because she felt that there was no other way for all the pain she was experiencing to stop. All too many people are in that same exact crazy, unfortunate position. They hate themselves, they hate their life, and they find no love for themselves or others.

God helped me; God lifted me up, loved me, and allowed me to love myself again. That is the greatest victory that you can get out of this war, out of this battle – that you can love again. But it starts with figuring out how to love yourself. Despite your circumstances or your situation, you too can begin to find JOY ON YOUR JOURNEY where you are right now.

FROM VICTIM TO VICTORIOUS:
FREE YOURSELF

A Voice for the Victim

Luke 6:45 ...out of the abundance of the heart the mouth speaks.

I have often been asked why I want to share what I went through. I have even been accused of wanting to live in the past. Who wants to relive such a thing? What do I get out of it? Is there a benefit for telling the world that something so sinister happened to me? My answer has always been and will always be that it is my hope, desire, and purpose to make sure that no other little girl has to go through that shame alone, and that the woman who hasn't dealt with this happening to her as a child will, too, become free from the bondage of the pain that she had no control to stop.

I recall a day that I went into my favorite local pizza joint looking to stuff my face. Since I make it a rule of engaging with at least five new people when I'm out, I greeted some young ladies having a girls night out. They invited me to sit down with them. We engaged in everyday conversations that lead to deeper conversations where I shared with them who I was and some of the things that I had experienced over the course of my life. As I shared with them in great detail about the molestation I went through one of the young ladies shared with me how she had gone through the same thing. She mentioned to me that she could never do what I was doing. She marveled that I was sharing my story on huge platforms and writing about what I had gone through. She then asked me to look her in her eyes and I will never forget what she said to me next. She asked me to write the hell out of this book for her and all the other women and young girls who will never be able to openly share their story because of fear, shame or judgement.

Certainly, we all handle the after care of trauma differently and I'm not suggesting that anyone should get on anybody's stage to tell their story if they don't feel lead to. However, I do suggest that you seek therapy, get spiritual guidance and truly begin to love yourself through the healing process.

I want every victim who is suffering from any kind of abuse to know that something beautiful can come from something so dark and ugly. I want them to know they have the power to let it continue to happen to them through their thoughts, or they can now bring it to silence through facing it, getting the help they need, and in turn, they can reach back and help the next one get through. I hope that those individuals who hear my story can, too, find their liberated voices and be free from whatever it was for them that may have caused them to be stuck in the past, and truly walk in freedom. I use my voice to speak out so that little girl, that teenager, or that grown woman knows that she has an advocate on her side who will reinforce that no, it was not your fault; no, you did not do anything wrong; and NO, what happened was not right or normal.

First, know that you cannot fix yourself alone and it does not happen instantaneously. God has been my source of strength but I also received counseling from my pastor who took the time, listened and fed me spiritual knowledge. I had friends and even strangers who poured something into me. This process to healing had many steps and has been years in the making. I encourage all victims of abuse to seek out a spiritual or licensed professional. The remainder of this book details what I have done throughout the years to help myself grow and find my joy. The stages to joy for me included letting the pain out and telling my story (which I am still doing), as well as doing what I call "D.A.M.A.G.E. Control" and overcoming the damage. Finally, I constantly take steps to access my joy. It is an never-ending course of action.

D.A.M.A.G.E. CONTROL

Most people experience some type of damage in their lives growing up. That damage can be physical, spiritual, financial, or emotional. The bottom line is that damage is something that very few people escape in life. Old television shows like the Cosby Show and the Brady Bunch showed us a lifestyle in a world very far away from the reality that most of us lived. The parents on those shows were really awesome, and we all would have loved to be in any of those families. For most of us, the reality was no one had that type of fairytale functional family life. Every household in America has some type of dysfunction within it.

The struggle and the difficulty I faced with molestation at the hand of my father, was something that I will have to deal with for the rest of my life. But if I allow it to become the focal point of my life, my life will lose value, meaning and JOY. The JOY that I have today helps me see the damage that I have overcome, and go beyond.

I discovered that in order to have the right amount of JOY for the journey, you need to be able to make the damage as slight as possible. I didn't have the answers when I was a little girl, or even in my early adult years, that could help me get through or begin the healing process when the abuse was over. Now God has given me strategies to help other individuals who need some help becoming unstuck behind the thing that caused them paralyzing damage. Too many people allow the damage to define their lives and determine who they are or what they will become. I have decided to do damage control. Damage control is a six-step process, which will help others take control over the damage in their lives. I created the acronym to help me through the process.

The first step to engage in damage control is to

D - Dream Big. To keep the damage that life throws at us from controlling us, we have to have a dream that's bigger than the pain that the damage causes.

To *Dream Big* means that we see something beyond our immediate boundaries. We see a life of possibility, of potential, of something more than what we're experiencing right now. Most people have experienced, are experiencing, or will experience difficulty and delay. When we *Dream Big* we see pass that delay and disappointment. Instead, we see a positive alternative to that negative reality. We *Dream Big* by seeing where we are, we say where we want to be, we envision a future that has everything that we desire, and we take the necessary steps to promote the manifestation of what we see for ourselves.

Dreaming Big starts with, number one, knowing exactly what it is that we want.

"Shoot for the moon, because even if you miss, you will land among the stars." *Les Brown*

The world is saddled with too many people that have aimed low and hit, not realize that they could have aimed higher and gotten even more. To *Dream Big* means that we see something beyond our immediate boundaries, we see something beyond our immediate scope of possibility, and we see something that seems to be impossible to the average person.

To *Dream Big* means that you are willing to get outside of the box, outside of that comfort zone, and strive for something better even if that something seems out of reach. It becomes within reach when we decide to allow it to manifest itself. To *Dream Big* means that we see something that we want and are willing to go after it, even though it seems as if we don't have the capacity or the ability to achieve it.

What's your dream? Is it bigger than what the damage was? When we get caught up in focusing on the damage rather than on the dream, we get stuck. Too many people are stuck and don't realize it because they have stopped *Dreaming Big;* in most cases, they've stopped dreaming at all.

The next step to engage in damage control is to

A - Ask Often. The Bible tells us in James 4:3 that we have not because we ask not and with wrong motives. If you are like me, you hate asking anyone for anything for fear of being rejected, but I had to learn that a closed mouth doesn't get fed. First of all, it's okay to ask our father who is in heaven. *Asking Often* means that we call on our ultimate source, God, to make our request known. It's also okay to ask others; they will either be able to help you out or they won't.

As long as your intentions are clear, honest, and you are not operating out of a manipulative spirit, it is okay to have "no" as the answer. *Asking Often* just says that your dream has validity. As such, we have the authority, the ability, and the responsibility to be able to request that it be made manifest. All too often, we suffer in lack because we ask not.

We have to realize that what we ask for has the ability and the possibility of becoming a reality.

Asking is the primary key that opens the door to possibility. "A closed mouth doesn't get fed" – you want to be able to trust the process of asking for the help or guidance you need to help you move forward. To make sure that the damage is kept under control, we have to *Ask Often* for what we want.

The next step to engage in damage control is to

M - Mention Daily those things that we need and want to manifest in our lives. Mention that thing you desire. Mentioning it daily allows whatever you are trying to stabilize in your life to resonate in your spirit, your heart, dreams or desires. Those are the things that we pray and meditate on.

Philippians 4:8 And now, dear brothers and sisters one final thing. Fix your thoughts on what is true, and honorable, and right and pure, and lovely and admirable. Think about things that are excellent and worthy of praise.

If you think about the positive alternative, that becomes that reality in our lives. If we want to see more of what we desire, we need to focus on and *Mention* that daily. Every day, we have to wake up with the dream, with the desire in our spirit; we have to take the time to allow it to resonate with our spirit. Allow it to be able to become a focus of our spirit, a focus of our heart.

What you meditate on becomes the abundance of your heart. If what you're speaking is not what you're seeking, you may be *Mentioning* the wrong thing.

I've learned over time that when you Mention and focus on that what you want, it will manifest – whether it is positive or negative.

I found myself early on mentioning the acts of abuse and molestation that had begun to confine and define my life. That constant mentioning caused me to lose hope and become angry, frustrated, alienated, and polarized. I looked at my life as something that was unattractive, that was shameful and embarrassing. The more I mentioned it the more it not only came into my life, but it prevented me from being able to move on with my life.

At some point, I began to realize that mentioning those negative, nasty debilitating things was what was causing them to remain in my life. I realized I had to figure out a way to bring some positivity out of what happened to me. This is why I tell my story now, to help other individuals who are going through or have gone through the same things I have, and even worse.

Positively *Mention* daily the things that we want to focus on. That is what causes success and blessings to occur.

A - Answer Truthfully. We often try to hide our shame from the world. The damage that has been done to us over the course of our lives causes us to want to hide the truth about it because it is so ugly. In order to find JOY on the journey, you have to begin to *Answer Truthfully* what hurts you or what keeps you from fully moving forward. I like to say, "tell the truth and shame the devil." By that I mean don't allow your truth to be spoken by anyone else because they will not tell it the way that it needs to be told. In other words, let it come "straight from the horse's mouth!"

To deny the damage, to deny the hurt, the pain, the frustration, is to delay the healing. To deny it causes it to become more entrenched. Denial is an emotional response, a coping mechanism that tries to hide the truth. In order to find JOY, we must *Answer Truthfully*. We must answer the questions that are put before us by our own minds or by others.

The truth is that we were abused; the truth is that we were hurt; the truth may be that we don't want anything to do with the abuser ever again. To answer that in no uncertain terms allows us to get beyond the abuse. To state that these actions happened, but we are not going to allow them to define us, to confine us, or to prevent us from being able to move forward, is the key to putting more JOY in your life. JOY is significant in your continuing to move forward.

People, places, and things can make us happy for periods of time. JOY is not circumstantial; it is not just what is going on. JOY is something that we all have on the inside of us, and only leaves us when we give it away. We have to make up in our minds and understand that God gave us this JOY, and no one can take it away. I want you to know that all you have to do is decide and choose to be JOYFUL, JOYOUS AND FREE.

When we answer ourselves authentically and truthfully, we allow ourselves to heal. The healing begins with dealing with the truth. To deny the reality of what occurred only causes that to continue to control us. When we answer truthfully to ourselves and to others, we allow ourselves to face and confront the issue and move beyond it.

The JOY for the journey is what allows us to have the energy, the stamina, and the fuel to make it through to the destination that GOD has planned for us.

G - Give Consistently in order to guarantee joy for the journey. *Give* away some of your time, share your talent, and bless others with your treasure. *Give* in such a way that it allows you to find the JOY in giving.

Acts 20:35 In everything I did, I showed you that by this kind of hard work must help the weak, remembering the words the Lord Jesus himself said: It is more blessed to give than to receive.

Too many people find themselves unwilling, or feeling like they are unable, to *Give* because they are trying to hold on to the little that they do have. As a result of that, they find themselves having even less. The JOY of giving is that it exposes the fact that you have more than you need. If you have more than you need, there is no problem sharing it with others, and for greater causes.

On your journey to JOY, victory, and success, it's necessary that you *Give* out of your abundance. Abundance really is a state of mind.

Giving is not always about what you can give physically in the way of material things, either. It's about giving words that encourage, time that you can't get back, and love that causes impact.

When you operate in the avenue of abundance, it means that you realize that your needs aren't that great, that there is enough in your life to sustain and satisfy everything that you need. Then there's leftover, there's abundance, excess that you can share with your circle of humanity, the community, and the kingdom at large. Sometimes just giving to another person or giving to a good cause can cause us feelings of peace and a reward that can only come from God.

E - Expect Great, is the final step in D.A.M.A.G.E control and, in my opinion, the most exciting part of all. We don't regularly give much thought to our expectations. For example, when we walk into a dark room, we don't even realize that we have an expectation that when we flip the light switch, illumination occurs in that space. In other instances, we are fully aware of our expectations of others. For example, when a person tells you that they are going to call you back at a certain time, you fully *Expect* that person to call you. Some of our most significant expectations are those we have for ourselves. It doesn't matter where the expectation comes from; it matters how we manage those expectations in our pursuits to finding and keeping JOY on our journeys.

When a woman is going through a pregnancy, they say she's expecting. There is an expectation that at an appointed time, delivery will take place. That delivery will produce a new life with new possibilities; ultimately, a new person is coming into the world. Pregnant women know this expectancy and look forward to and prepare for that appointed time. That time generally is nine months, and at the end of that nine-months, either by induction or natural delivery a baby is born.

That same expectation should occur in your life; you should *Expect Great* things to happen. That expectancy is what will allow you to go through the difficult times, to go through the times that have caused you to be damaged and feel less than your personal best.

Expect more, *Expect JOY, Expect* success. I WILL CAUTION YOU not to allow your expectancy to turn into pressure. If we *Expect* to win a race, we put pressure on ourselves to do so, and often through very extreme measures. That pressure can either work for us or against us. When the pressure is motivating us, we can focus, put goals into a perspective that we can reach, and take a look at potential obstacles. Pressure can work against you and cause feelings of anxiety and failure as well. Make sure that you have a clear and well-thought-out process for your level of expectancy. The expectancy is heightened when your talent isn't working for you, or the depth of lack is overwhelming, and your excess is gone.

On this journey we call life, *Expect Great* JOY to show up and remain in spite of the pain. JOY is knowing that even though circumstances have beaten you down and have caused you to get off track, you can get back on track when you keep your JOY intact. That is what allowed me to go from damage to deliverance. Following and applying any of the strategies that I have shared with you in this book will help you, too, to begin a life of freedom that will lead you in not only finding JOY on your journey, but also in enjoying the journey!

Steps to Help Overcome DAMAGE

Psalm 34:19 The righteous person may have many troubles, but the Lord delivers him from them all.

I was able to overcome and survive something that no child should have ever been exposed to. I was able to overcome and survive it because I developed a system along with God that allowed me to be able to stand in the midst of my struggle and overcome in the midst of my obstacle.

The thing that I would love for you as the reader to take away from this book is that you hold all the power you need to be set free, and the ability to move forward. You do not have to be in bondage for years and years behind something you had no control over or power to stop.

When people are damaged, they are unable to perform at their best. They're not able to deliver what they were designed to deliver. Take sports, for example. If you got hurt or "damaged" during a game, you would be put on the injured reserve list. That states that they know that you have the skills, that you possess the ability for the team, but that you have been sidelined with an injury and damage that is preventing you from being able to get on the field to play and do what you and the coaching team knows you can do.

I'd like to share with you a simple system that I've employed to be able to recognize and overcome the damages that life sometimes can put upon you. No one said life would be easy, but it is easier to overcome when you have a system in place. The reason you need a system is because you have to know which steps you're employing, and which steps are missing if success is not manifesting itself.

My system begins with and utilizes the letters in the word DAMAGE. Since damage is what got me to the point where I was unable to function and move forward consistently, God and I put an acronym together with a positive spin on the word "DAMAGE."

I'm a simple person. I look at life as something to be lived, loved, and learned from. In the process of living, certain things happen that we don't foresee. Some of these things, I will admit, are our own fault, and others are a result of other people not caring, being selfish or greedy. We can't change everybody, but we can change ourselves. This simple system is a way to really focus on what's important and achieve the results that we want to see manifest in our lives. I hope that you see the word DAMAGE a bit differently after you have read the meaning of our acronym for it.

1. Declare

Our first point is that you have to DECLARE some things. Before a thing can be established, you have to DECLARE it. It is amazing how the words we use shape our lives. The more you speak, hear or read words, they become more powerful over you, and you at some point begin to believe what's being deposited into the receptive part of your brain. DECLARE that the past is over, that it is done with, and that it no longer controls you! The biggest problem we face with moving forward is that we don't know how to speak to our problems.

Proverbs 18:21 The tongue has the power of life and death, and those who love it will eat of its fruit.

Instead of speaking life, we are speaking death over our own selves. I don't think it's on purpose; we have been conditioned at early ages to say things like "I'm so sick of you," "I can't," or "I'm so clumsy," and we say these things with no regard to the negative energy we are releasing that ultimately affects us physically.

Some of us are in the terrible habit of repeating over and over the same negative words, and the problem is this: our brains use repetition, patterns, and consistency to learn. Remember when you were learning how to add or multiply? You used repetition, patterns, and consistency and it's forever etched into the thought process of your brain. You never have to think about the answer to 2x2; you automatically know the answer is 4.

For every negative word spoken, you have to say a thousand positive words to begin to erase the negative. Sure, some very uncomfortable, unkind, and unnecessary things happened to me and it happens to people all over the world every day.

When we react, it is in support of our defensive nature. We seem to be at a disadvantage because we are uncomfortable with what has been said or done to us. Our emotions take a central control. The downside to reacting is that we let emotions without reasons drive us forward and we lose control. Simply put, reacting is sporadic and emotional.

The flip side of this is to respond. Responding is more thoughtful, and our responses contain reasoning.

Responding is guided less by emotions and more by our logic. However, a response is more active, and it can change the trajectory of any conversation. The benefit of responding is that it's positive, civil, and it offers us the opportunity to grow. In declaring that the past is past, we get a chance to not be controlled by the occurrences of the past.

The declaration that the past is an event that has already occurred and not one that is occurring now is powerful. It releases us from the tentacles and the anchors of the past that held us stuck and are trying to prevent us from moving forward. You see, the power of the past is that it reminds us constantly of what happened and reminds us constantly that we are controlled by what happened.

When you DECLARE that the past no longer is active, that it no longer has control or power over you, it allows you to be able to stand up and to move forward past the struggle, past what had you stuck, and into a future that you get to determine and declare on your own. That liberation, that very action of speaking what you want rather than what you have encountered, is what gives you that next leverage, that next step up toward the goals and dreams that you have for yourself.

Many people want a better life, and yet they are stuck in a bad life that happened as a result of the past. The actions that got you stuck in the first place are actions that you did not approve of, that you find to be disgusting, deplorable, or not in your best interest. We find ourselves stuck because we allow those actions to continue to control us and hold us.

The very act of DECLARING that the past is just that, the past, is the first step to liberate yourself from the actions that are causing you disease. It's easy to keep walls built around you and stay in isolation, but that's not what God wants for you.

This simple action of DECLARING that what happened to you is over and that event is no longer active allows us to be able to move forward without hindrance. There are so many of us are walking around with past hurts, unable to move forward on the path that God designed for us. No one wants to be stuck; no one wants to be beaten, raped or abused in any way, but the sad fact is that it happens. If you are that person who has been the victim, DECLARE right now with me that "I am no longer a victim! I am a strong, resilient, victorious person and I am taking control of my life!"

Once that is done, you can get on with the next steps to designing the life that you truly deserve and desire.

What are some areas you wish to make
DECLARATIONS over your life? Write them down
and look back over them as the days go by, so you
have a reminder on your journey to finding and
keeping your JOY!

_____

_____

_____

_____

_____

_____

DAMAGED 2 Delivered

---

2. Acknowledge

ACKNOWLEDGE what you want to achieve. All too often, people express and articulate what they don't want. Science has proven that if we focus on what we don't want, we will get more of what we don't want. Most people are so focused on reliving, retelling, and resenting what occurred that they don't give any energy or focus to what they do want to occur. That is a fundamental fact.

I want you to begin to ACKNOWLEDGE what you want, what you desire, what you deserve. The basic form of ACKNOWLEDGING is speaking or writing it.

Habakkuk 2:2 And the Lord answered me: Write the vision; make it plain on tablets, so he may run who reads it.

Write down the vision for your life so you can see it and take off running with it, so you can bring it to fruition. No matter what it is that you may want – if you want a better relationship, a better job, better fellowship, better times – we need to concentrate on speaking that, then that becomes our reality.

Our reality is defined by what we decide to put a focus on. When I was going through the hard areas of my life, I remember speaking to myself as I watched shows like Good Times, The Brady Bunch, or the Cosby Show and wished that I was Thelma, Cindy, or Rudy. What I was envisioning was a life where there was no abuse, with a TV dad that loved his daughter, me.

On those shows, I saw a me that wasn't being traumatized, and although it was not my reality, it helped me see what I wanted nonetheless. As I got older and the realization began to set in that what was happening to me was not normal, I wanted more and more to have a life that was that was nice and not naughty. I wanted a life filled with all the love, care, and protection I saw on those shows.

That second step is to ACKNOWLEDGE what you want and to articulate that desire. What you speak is what you seek. What you say is what you will see manifested. If you continually speak of the negative aspects of your life, the negative parts will remain, and the negative forces will make sure that your focus of negativity will be perpetuated. Instead, you must learn to speak positivity into your life. Be exact about what you want in your life. Believing God for a home, family, or a great career doesn't come by only believing – you have to speak life over it as if it's already done for you. The idea is to express, speak, and ACKNOWLEDGE the many positive alternatives, and no longer speak or ACKNOWLEDGE negative.

Many of us face negative realities. Some of us have been fired, some have lost loved ones, and sadly, some have experienced the trauma and the drama that I went through as a little girl. But just because you dealt with those disappointing and depressing experiences doesn't mean that you have to live that for the rest of your life. By expressing the negative, we are returning to that and keeping it at the forefront of our minds.

The end result of that activity is a life stuck in a place, in a mold that we don't want. So, from this point forward, my recommendation is that you ACKNOWLEDGE what you want to achieve and receive, and what you want or don't want to manifest. I'm not going to tell you that everything will miraculously be picture-perfect, but I will tell you that you will have your peace, love, and JOY, and you will see a better life begin to manifest for you.

What are the areas you need to ACKNOWLEDGE in your life?

_____

_____

_____

_____

_____

_____

_____

_____

_____

3. Meditate

The third point is you have to MEDITATE on what you want to manifest in your life. It goes hand-in-hand with acknowledging what you want; however, it must be repeated over and over and over again in the thought process which will come through MEDITATION. That repetition of continually MEDITATING on what you want to see manifested in your life is what will cause it to manifest. Having it written down and placed where you can see it every day, like on your mirror or on a vision board that you create, will help you keep "the main the main thing."

In essence, MEDITATION will help the process of removing the negative energy that will try to continue to come around you. MEDITATION doesn't take copious amounts of time to do, and has several benefits that I want to bring to your attention. The most common benefit of MEDITATION is that it reduces stress; even five minutes can provide a significant decrease in stress. According to the *American Heart Association*, MEDITATING is also good for your cardiovascular health and can reduce the risk of cardiovascular disease. According to the

Mayo Clinic, meditation can also reduce high blood pressure.

Many styles of MEDITATION focus on regulating and being aware of how you breathe. This allows you to clear your mind and release tension that is locked up in your body. There are many reasons why MEDITATION is beneficial to the body, and one of my favorite benefits is that it reduces pain. As a person who experiences pain 24/7, MEDITATION has helped reduce the extreme level of pain I was experiencing before I started MEDITATING. My testimony is this: I was on a total of four different prescribed pain medications simultaneously for about ten years. Two of them were narcotics. Needless to say, I was always very lethargic; I could barely get out of bed. After having a talk with God, I took myself off all those pain medications and implemented the art of MEDITATION into my daily life which has proven for me to be an aid in getting through the excruciating pain associated with the complications of diabetes.

Enough cannot be said about MEDITATION and focusing on what you want, rather than what you don't. I'm convinced that there is a law of manifestation that comes from the universe – when you focus on a thing, the universe rewards us by manifesting exactly what we put our major focus on. Sadly, the universe will give you more of the pain and frustration and disappointment that you don't want if you continue to meditate on those things to the point of making them part of your reality, when it really is not supposed to be.

Case in point: a woman that is with an abusive person leaves him and finds that she is always ending up with that type of individual. Because she continues to meditate on the fact that the type of man she always gets turns out to be abusive, that is what she will always attract into her life.

I've adopted the daily practice of not speaking of the negative realities that exist around me; instead, I only meditate on the positive alternatives. As I begin to meditate on what I want manifested, I've seen a great relationship develop when it seemed like there was no one there for me. I've seen opportunities come from seemingly nowhere because I was MEDITATING and speaking and acknowledging that that's what I wanted in my life.

Get in the habit of MEDITATING on a regular basis on what you want to see manifested, rather than on the problem you don't want to see manifested in your life. As a result of MEDITATING and consistently speaking life, you will, like me, begin to see all of the positive alternatives that God has designed for your life.

What are 5 areas of your life you can MEDITATE on, believing for positive manifestation?

1._____

2._____

3._____

4._____

5._____

4. Accept

The fourth point is that you have to ACCEPT forgiveness for yourself. Forgiveness is not for the other person, although they DO benefit. Forgiveness is for you. As long as you hold on to the hurt, you do nothing but rehearse the hurt. That hurt becomes a stuck point for you. It will not allow you to move on. As long as you are remembering and rehearsing and dictating the information of the incident that caused you to not forget, you will stay stuck in that incident. You will be paralyzed by that reality that existed and happened so long ago.

No, I'm not saying give a free pass to the person who abused you and caused you pain; rather, I'm saying give yourself a free pass to get past it. No longer let it hold you and prevent you from moving forward. ACCEPT forgiveness for yourself. ACCEPTING forgiveness is an act that says I no longer hold onto this, but I release it so it no longer controls my life. And as a result, the person who perpetrated the pain will be forgiven by you, and you leave them to deal their actions.

People know when they are doing things that are not nice, that are not right. They do them anyway. Why, you ask? Because it feels good to them; it gives them power. It allows them to get away with something for a time. But over time, it eats away at them. Your forgiveness is the greatest punishment that they could possibly receive, because they know they hurt you, they know they abused you, they know that what they did to you wasn't right.

The Bible talks of putting hot coals on the head of people by forgiving them, because now they are required to deal with what they did. Don't hold them captive any longer, because in reality you are the real captive. By releasing others, it releases you to be free and to accept everything that was designed for you. That one action will reverse the damage, set you free, and end the pain. Of course, it's easier said than done, but not impossible. You definitely have to put in the work.

In which areas do you need to ACCEPT Forgiveness?

_____

_____

_____

_____

_____

_____

_____

_____

_____

5. Give

The fifth step is to GIVE. It's important to GIVE forgiveness to others. I have at times thought that it was selfish of me to accept forgiveness for something I didn't cause in the first place. I now know that's not true. It's a selfish thought to want forgiveness and turn around and not GIVE that same forgiveness to someone who has done you wrong. Sometimes, for us to accept that forgiveness for self is difficult to do, depending on how deeply the roots are attached to your issue. In my opinion, though, it's even more important to GIVE forgiveness to others. Let's be honest, the individual that damaged you, raped you, abused you, stole from you, or cheated on you doesn't deserve forgiveness from you, but the bible says otherwise:

Matthew 6:14 For if you forgive other people when they sin against you, your heavenly Father will also forgive you.

I don't know about you, but I need the Lord's forgiveness for some wrongs that I've done. Furthermore, I believe that giving and granting forgiveness to others makes you a stronger, more loving, better person, and it opens the door for you to be able to become who you were designed to be. Harboring hatred, harboring hurt, harboring the pain will not change what happened. It only manifests and magnifies in your life more and causes more damage longer.

If you want the damage to be over, if you want to survive it and overcome it, you must GIVE forgiveness to those that caused the pain in the first place. By accepting forgiveness and giving forgiveness, you will experience freedom like you never have before, and you will open the door for your victory.

Who and for what do you need to forgive? What is it that you need to accept forgiveness for? 10 spaces are provided for you below but be honest with yourself. If your list exceeds 10, go ahead and get additional paper.

1._____

2._____

3._____

4._____

5._____

6._____

7._____

8._____

9._____

10._____

6. Establish

The sixth and final point is you must ESTABLISH boundaries. As a little girl, I wasn't able to ESTABLISH boundaries. My abuser was able to come into my bedroom to get me away in unsafe places and take advantage of me. I was not able to set boundaries, to keep him from coming to get me, so I had to go through what I went through. I had to deal with the pain and abuse. Every time that it happened, it scared me more and more, but I have forgiven him and I have DECLARED that the past is the past and I will no longer be controlled by it.

As a child I had no authority, no power, no ability to set those boundaries. But as an adult, as a mature person, as a conscious individual that has control over my life, I can now control those boundaries and set those boundaries and prevent the abuse from taking place ever again. With ESTABLISHING boundaries, you create a level of protection for yourself and you reduce the chances of being taken advantage of by anyone going forward.

But you have to know what those boundaries are and be clear when you set them, so that others will not take advantage of the fact that you may have not been serious because you have never set boundaries before. That's okay, stand your ground and demand that respect. By ESTABLISHING boundaries, you give yourself permission to be protected, permission to get be back in control.

As I look back on the pain that became deeply rooted on the inside of me, I'm so glad to finally have a system in place that will allow me to never again play the part of a victim, but always be victorious. My goal is to share what I have learned along this journey in finding JOY with as many women as possible so that I can help them to establish those boundaries, overcome, and survive the damage that they've had in their lives.

Damage that has left them shattered, in pain, struggling, and not knowing how to survive. Survival begins the moment you take back control of your life. To rehearse the pain, to continue to acknowledge the abuse and the abuser doesn't do anything positive for your situation. Use this six-step system to get you started. You may want or need to add to what I have started, but the point is to get started doing something that will aid you in moving forward, getting past the pain, and maintaining a healthy and victorious life. Nothing can stop you unless you allow it to. When we become mature adults, we become individuals who have our own destiny in our own hands. Then we are able to make sure that no one invades the areas in our lives that are personal to us without our consent, and we are in control of our lives again.

I ACCEPT forgiveness for myself. I MEDITATE on the positive that I want to see in my life a regular basis. I ACKNOWLEDGE what I want to see manifested in my life. I GIVE forgiveness more quickly now because I do need my heavenly father's forgiveness. Now I'm able to ESTABLISH boundaries.

What boundaries do you need to ESTABLISH in your life?

_____

_____

_____

_____

_____

_____

_____

_____

_____

DAMAGED 2 Delivered

Parenting As A Victim of Abuse

I have to acknowledge I may have been unfair to my children when they were young. I was an overprotective parent because I knew what I had been through and how I lashed out. I did not want the same for my children. Your reasons for being an overprotective parent to your children may not be the result of abuse. Still, I have a few suggestions based on my experience as a young parent:

1. You have to be present in your children's lives, but do not be overbearing. They need space to grow, figure things out, and become who they are created to be in this world.

2. Try not to place your fears onto your children. Inform them and give them the tools they need to succeed, and leave it there. The rest is in God's hands. Trust Him.

3. This is not easy, but you have to remove some of the emotion from the equation when dealing with your kids, whatever their age, so that they can move on and develop to the next levels of maturity. Remind yourself that at some point in the parent-child relationship, what they say or do is not a reflection on you. Yes, that's your child, your baby or your "lil' peanut," but lil' peanut is going to grow up and have lil' peanuts, too, and you do not want to raise adults that need a crutch for the rest of their lives. You don't want to create a negative cycle that could continue into the next generation.

4. Ask questions, but do not give them the third degree. You cannot fire off twenty questions in three minutes and expect detailed answers for each of those questions right in that moment. Ease up and let them (at times) feel like they are in control of the flow of the conversation. They need to know that you have trust in them. Once they know that, they will come to you freely. The goal here is to help your children with communicating, but allow them at the same time an opportunity to think for themselves, which will help them feel like they have some control over their own lives.

5. Don't position yourself as a needy parent! Stand on your own two feet! I'm joking, but I'm not! You don't "need" your children to like you. Validation that you are an amazing mother or father from your children should not be needed...appreciated, yes, but not needed. As soon as they see that you need them to survive, you place yourself in a vulnerable position because they don't have to fully comply, and that vulnerability takes away the natural respect and power you have as a parent.

When you need something and you don't get it, you naturally try harder to get it by controlling and manipulating the situation, which is what I totally did with my daughter and I'm telling you it backfired. I needed her to understand that what I did as her parent was totally for her good. When she didn't get it, I pushed harder for her to get it, which backfired on me.

6. Respond, don't react! This will take some work for most of you who are parents of teenagers. They will try you. Some of them feel like they know more than you do as the parent, but you are the one that's the adult, so send them to their rooms so you both have a chance to calm down. Once you both are calm, you can then talk and resolve whatever the conflict was.

The biggest and most daunting aspect of having gone through the type of abuse or trauma that I experienced is the realization that you can prevent those around you from living because you're trying so hard to make sure they don't experience the same thing. Hear me clearly: when you take the posture that you are going to "save them all," you run the risk of losing much of your sanity, your peace, and the one that you are trying to save. I was very close to all three of those aspects becoming reality in my life.

Smothering my daughter was a result of me not knowing my own worth even as a mother, or who I was supposed to be in the role of the mother. To say that I was obsessive would be an utter understatement.

The laser focus that I had on her caused much delay in my own progression into the woman that I was designed to be from the beginning. Instead, I ended up creating a negative life for her that was just as oppressive as my own.

In my daughter's teenage years, I wanted to create an environment for her and her girlfriends that would allow them a place where they could have transparent conversations, fellowship, and encourage one another.

I wanted them to build a sisterhood. At that time in my life, I had five friends that were and are still to this day individuals that I know have my back and I have theirs, and I thought it important for the girls to establish that type of relationship amongst their group.

One of my daughter's sister friends actually approached me about meeting with them at that time once a month, and I agreed. At the time, they all viewed me as a woman of wisdom. Little did they know I was still struggling with my past demons. I was still in grizzly bear mode when it came to the protection of my daughter. I even basked in the compliments that were always given during that time about how I looked like my daughter's sister and not her mother, which I loved; my daughter, well not so much. To me that meant that it was okay for me to hang with my daughter and her friends because everyone thought I was one of them.

I didn't know how to stop being an overprotective mom, which eventually caused there to be a huge falling out between all of the girls and myself. One of them said something negative about my daughter and I was not having that. I told you previously that I would fight anybody for all of my children. Unfortunately for my daughter, it ruined a few of her sister friendships. Looking back and now understanding more about myself, my interference during that time is one of my biggest regrets.

I have never had a desire to do or be a part of anything that pertained to women's ministry. I didn't like women because "we" have a tendency to be gossipy, cat fighters, and seemingly hard to get along with for long periods of time. Needless to say, most of my friends were guys. Even now it's like that, but I have made adjustments within myself over the years to build sister relationships with women.

After the monthly meetings with the girls failed, I still felt the Lord tugging on me to start a women's ministry. I looked into my own life and thought that it was impossible for me to stand before anybody, least of all a bunch of women that I wanted nothing to do with in the first place, and speak. I felt I had nothing of any value to tell women because I was such a broken woman myself. I never had the innocence of childhood, never had the opportunity to know what it was truly like to be a baby girl much less a grown woman.

What in the world would I say? How could I offer encouragement when I was so discouraged? *God*, I asked, *is this truly what you want of me?* I found answers in the bible, and it became clear that there was an assignment on my life that was by God's design before I was a dot in my mother's womb.

1 Jeremiah 1:5 Before I formed you in the womb I knew you, before you were born I set you apart; I appointed you as a prophet to the nations. NIV

This scripture helped me to begin to see my worth. I am enough. I am strong. I am beautiful. I can, and I *will* do whatever He wants me to do when He wants me to do. I am a Queen on an assignment. God has equipped me with this JOY and love that I know could only come from Him, to ignite, invoke and impact the lives of those I cross paths with to see that their JOY is significant and to help them get through whatever struggles that they may be battling with.

Realizing that I am a Queen and that I belong to God helps me to help others realize their worth as Queens and Kings also. One of the major things that God showed me about myself is that He is using me for His glory, and that I truly imitate the love of Christ. I willingly show that love to all I come in contact with. Am I saying that I'm perfect? Absolutely not! I have messed up some relationships, but I am of the belief that when you know better, you do better. So right now, today, I truly treat people the way I want to be treated, so much so that if there is anyone that has been hurt by me in any way, I TRULY APOLOGIZE FROM THE BOTTOM OF MY HEART and I would be willing to revisit the relationship. I realize that hurt people hurt other people when they don't deal with what hurt them.

7 Steps to Accessing Your Joy

Psalm 30:5 For His anger endureth but a moment, and in His favor is life; weeping may endure for a night, but joy cometh in the morning.

Over the years, I have had to figure out how to not only access my JOY but *keep* my JOY. That resolve only came through my relationship with God. What I am about to share with you are seven 7 tips that have helped me on my journey to truly finding JOY. I call them "My Roadmap To JOY," and you can have them as your own, too.

1. *Let Go of Negativity!*
   - See every challenge as an opportunity for elevation and growth.
   - Be grateful for all you have, knowing that somebody somewhere wishes they had half of what you are blessed to have.
   - Be optimistic about the future and your ability to achieve your goals. Things will not always be the same. Weeping may endure for a night, but JOY comes in the morning.
   - Open your mind to success and embrace failure/mistakes that have happened along the way. It is all part of the journey.
   - Begin a practice of taking "worry vacations" where you train your mind not to worry for a certain length of time. Start with a few minutes a day and add additional minutes every day. Before you know it, negative things that worried you before will not affect you the same. You will then be a master of how to not worry.

- If you want to be a positive person, you have to get around positive people and positive energy. Positivity is infectious, and you will be grateful you caught it.
- Don't take life so seriously. Know that it's okay to laugh even at yourself. Find reasons to just laugh!

2. *Keep A Servant's Heart and Always Be Kind.*
   - Treat everyone with kindness. Not only does it help others to feel better, but you will notice that you too will feel better after positive interactions with others. Remember to always treat people the way that you want to be treated.
   - Speak well of others. When you speak negatively of others, you will attract more negativity to yourself. It's simple:

3. *The Law of Attraction: Positivity will attract positivity.*
   - Truly listen to others. Be present and attentive to what others are really saying when they speak. Try to support them without bringing yourself into it (this can be difficult; take it one conversation at a time).
   - Be careful with your words. Speak gentler, kinder, and wiser.
   - Respect others and their free will.
   - Be open to trusting others, and you will be trusted in return. Enjoy the sense of community and friendship that comes from the openness and truth in one another.

- Practice generosity and giving without expecting anything in return. Involve yourself with service opportunities and offer what you can to a greater cause.
- Smile more – to family, to co-workers, to neighbors, to strangers inside Walmart, and watch it not only change how they, feel but also how you feel as well.

4. *Live in the present!*
   - Do not continue replaying negative events in your head or worrying about what the future holds. Trust God and allow Him to lead, guide, and direct you in the way that you should go. (Proverbs 3:5-6)
   - Be grateful for your life, for each and every moment of every day. Observe the constant and natural flow of change that surrounds us in your small yet important part in the natural, divine flow of life.
   - Observe yourself in the moment. Work on responding and not reacting. Often, it is best to step away before giving an answer. Honestly, this is something that I still work on daily.

5. *Choose a healthy lifestyle.*
   - Keep a daily routine. Wake up at the same time every morning, preferably early. Setting yourself to a natural biorhythm (any regular recurring motion, rhythm) will make it easier to wake up and feel energized.
   - Get enough sleep. Proper sleep is linked to POSITIVITY/POSITIVE PERSONALITY, improved characteristics like optimism, social

engagement, self-esteem, and even problem solving. *Proverbs 3:24 When you lie down, you will not be afraid; when you lie down your sleep will be sweet NASB.*

- Turn off the television. There is a life to be lived beyond the flat screen. Reader's Digest editors say that for every hour you sit in front of your television, you may be reducing your life expectancy by 22 minutes.
- Eat properly. What you eat has a direct effect on your mood and energy levels. Fill up on plenty of organically and locally grown fruits and vegetables, fish and poultry, nuts and whole grains. Don't overeat; try to practice self-control.
- Exercise daily, early in the morning preferably, to the point of sweating. It not only helps purify the body, but also releases endorphins, which helps in preventing stress, relieves depression, and positively improves your mind.
- Laugh more. Laughter is the best medicine. Like exercise, it releases endorphins that battle the negative effects of stress and promotes a sense of wellbeing and JOY.
- Practice DEEP BREATHING/MEDITATION. The body and mind are connected. Emotions affect the physical systems in the body, and the state of the body also affects the mind. By RELAXING & RELEASING tension through breathing/meditation practices, you feel calmer and centered throughout the day.

6. *Take Care of your Spirit!*

- Always strive to learn new things. Constantly expand your awareness and discover new ways of expressing your divine gifts.
- Get creative. It will help you discover new things, but will also keep your mind positive. Practice living in the moment, and allow your divine natural creativity to flow.
- PRACTICE MEDITATION. Research has proven that even as little as 10 minutes of meditation a day can lead to physical changes in the brain that improve concentration and focus, calms the nervous system, and helps you become a more kind, compassionate, and humorous individual. Meditation can also bring JOY and peace and love into your everyday life and activity.
- BE HONEST. Being honest alleviates a lot of unnecessary headache, aggravation, and wasted time. If you are honest with people, you give them the opportunity to decide if they want to continue on with you or how they will move forward with you. Telling the truth keeps you free inside, builds trust in relationships, and improves your willpower and the ability to attract success.
- Surrender ALL TO GOD and allow Him to take care of not only the greatest things in your life, but the smallest things as well. Remember you can do nothing without Him and everything with Him.

7. *Be free from the inside out.*

- Take time to better know yourself, family, friends, neighbors, and anyone that you profess to love or hold dear.
- Go without certain things that you think you want and consider whether they are needs or wants. If you find that something is a want and you can go without it, do that until you are able to get it without having to rob Peter to pay Paul. Go to new places where not everything is as easily accessible or readily available, and learn to appreciate what you have by expanding the world around you.
- DECLUTTER your mind and your home. Clutter is an unrecognized source of stress that promotes feelings of anxiety, frustration, distraction, and guilt. Feel good in your home; it is your sanctuary so keep it clean, organized, and JOYFUL.
- Live minimally and simply, not beyond your means. Extravagant living when you truly can't afford it often brings more stress, not satisfaction.

8. *Stay in a place of joy and peace.*
   - Be quick to forgive. Joy can be quickly restored if you learn how to simultaneously forgive and forget. God tells us He forgives our sins, puts them as far as the east is from the west and remembers them no more; take a look at Psalms 103:12 Isaiah 43:25
   - Take time every week to fill up your body's "gas tank." On weekends, escape to that place where you can feel peace so that you have a fresh start

to your week. Do exactly what you want without interruptions from anyone.

- Get extremely comfortable with yourself. Be confident in who God created you to be. Tall or short, thick or thin, pretty or not so pretty, be the BEST authentic you that you can be – yes, even with all of your perceived imperfections. Own your greatness it's all inside of you.

Live from the Inside Out

Proverbs 19:8 He who gets wisdom loves his own soul; he who keeps understanding will find good. NKJV

I heard Les Brown say, "You can't see the picture when you are in the frame." I can understand why he says this. For a long time, I couldn't see myself as anything other than scared, ugly, and useless. I couldn't see that I was God's masterpiece and He designed me and allowed me to experience the things that I did for His glory and His glory alone. He began to place me in and around people who helped me to see about myself what He saw. You see, while you are "in the frame," you can't see what everyone else sees. You have to literally get outside of yourself to see what God and others see.

God told me that I was beautiful, and it took Him using many random individuals who did not know me to tell me how beautiful, unique, and authentic I was for me to realize that YES, I am beautiful. I'm telling you that God wanted me to know my worth so much so, that he used this little old Caucasian woman who followed me through a grocery store while looking me up and down. As she did this, I remember thinking, *why is this woman following me through this store like this?* At some point, she stopped me and told me how beautiful I was and that I carried so much confidence when she saw me enter the store. God used that encounter with an individual who knew nothing about my inward struggle to make me realize the beauty that I possess, because all I could see was scars and ugliness. The scars will last a lifetime, scars that were making me feel disfigured and dishonored.

When God tells you that you are fearfully and wonderfully made, then the impossible becomes possible, "can't" turns into "can," and "won't" starts saying "I bet I will." You can begin at any time speaking life over your situation and your circumstances. Put that death tongue away and begin finding JOY on your journey.

I turned forty years old in September 2014. In December 2014, I had a talk with God as the count-down to a new year was going on. I looked up toward heaven I began to pray to God. The prayer included me saying to God that I did not want to do the next forty years of my life like I had done the first forty. It was in that moment that I started finding my true identity – who God created me to be, JOY.

Do not get me wrong, nothing happened overnight; however, there were and still are significant changes occurring in my life. In that moment, though, I can truly say that the chains of the bondage that I had felt for so long fell from me and I was set free. I was set free of negativity, self-doubt, and self-deprecation, and made to feel wonderful again.

For me, damage is something that happens on the inside of you. When you're damaged on the inside, people on the outside are confused about why you act a certain way, why you do a certain thing, why you engage in certain activities. Why is such a beautiful person engaging in such bad activities, bad actions? You are flawed, and they don't know why. They don't know the damage that you feel, that you experienced as a child. They don't know the taunting and teasing that you may have experienced from friends or from classmates. All they see is that outer shell that looks okay. I was not okay, and I needed to be okay. God finally gave me the guidance to become okay.

I was a mother that wasn't ready to be a parent. I was married too young at 17. I used parenting to blot out the pain and the shame of my past. I never truly felt protected by my parents. My friends, my boyfriend, my husband – I never found that security in any of them. I went into vigilante mode, never trusting anyone, never feeling that I was fully protected. The only way I found protection, peace, and power was in God. God was not looking at me and condemning me; instead, His word says there's no condemnation.

Romans 8: Therefore, there is now no condemnation for those who belong to Christ Jesus. NLT

I had belittled myself and hated myself as time went on, but my God has never left me nor forsaken me. God was and is the only one that has never turned His back on me, even when I have disappointed Him. Even now, it is because of Him that I can trust again and love individuals the way that I do. You can open up the door of trust to allow a better life to come in. Or you can keep the door closed and never allow anyone to come in because of fear of the past. I will say this: the ability to trust is a two-way door. Because of my behavior with different individuals, I have had to earn their trust again as well.

All too often, we put our negative experiences and situations in one big basket with a label on it stamped "bad things." We just keep them stored up way too long, hoping that no one will sneak a peek inside to see all the things that have happened to us because we don't know how to let people into our circle of trust. Not everyone is bad, but of course, not everyone is good. I had to learn how to let God put the people in my life that should be there, those are what I like to call divine connections. Sometimes we have to exclude even family members from the circle of trust. You see, it's not just the blood that flows through the veins, but it's the blood that flowed from Calvary's cross that allows us to be able to finally have the trust back in our lives.

John 11:4 When he heard this, Jesus said, "This sickness will not end in death. No, it is for God's glory so that God's Son may be glorified through it." NIV

I wanted to be done with the pain and the problems of the past; however, scars continued to afflict me throughout my life. At age 11 I was diagnosed with diabetes and told I would not make it to the age of 23. Throughout this battle, over the years I have been extremely sick at times. Over the past fifteen years, I have had non-stop pain, excruciating at times, in my legs, feet, and hands. Commonly called diabetic nerve damage, the medical term is *peripheral neuropathy,* which means weakness and pain from nerve damage. This, along with many other diabetic complications, has been very challenging for me, but I know that it has only been because of the grace and mercy of God that I'm still here.

In my lifetime, I have been told four times by doctors that they couldn't do anything else for me and I only had so much time to live. All glory to God, He has seen me through each and every one of those diagnoses. I know I am a walking miracle, and I am grateful.

As much as I would love to tell you that hearing those doctors tell me that I might not live much longer didn't upset me or that I kept my JOY, I can't. The first couple of times I freaked out, literally and figuratively. I've been told everything from *you are going to die by the time you are 31 weeks pregnant* (this was with my third child) to *we are going to have to amputate both of your feet.* Who has JOY after hearing anything like this? I did, after a while.

I want you to understand that at one point in my life, 2009 to be exact, I spent the majority of that year in the hospital. They had no clue at the time what was wrong with me. I was vomiting with diarrhea seven to eight days at a time non-stop. This would cause me to become dehydrated and I'd have to be rushed to the hospital, stay there five to seven days at a time, with IV's in both of my arms and hands. They would get me stable and send me home with nausea medicine. I would be home for two days, then the vomiting would start back up again, and I would have to be rushed back to the ER again. This went on for the entire year before they could tell me what was wrong with me. The diagnosis came from a doctor that was here from India who heard what was going on with me. He diagnosed me with gastroparesis – basically I don't digest my food within hours like most people do. Without medication and eating certain foods, whatever I eat on Monday will still be in my stomach on Saturday.

I have had so many surgeries on my legs and feet that I stopped keeping count as to how many. Everything that can be taken out of my body surgically except for my vital organs has been removed. Why am I telling you all of this? It's because I want you to see that I have all the reasons in the world to be angry and bitter about my life if I wanted to be. Yes, times have been hard to the point of me crying myself to sleep at night, not wanting to talk to anyone, or falling into deep depression, but that JOY down on the inside would always rise up in me and tell me, **no**! No, because there was something greater than all of the pain, sickness, hurt, and disappointment that I had been experiencing all of my life.

I believe that God with his infinite power wanted me to find and choose JOY. I now know that my JOY was significant to me getting up every day when the doctors said that I couldn't, despite hearing that I was not going to make it to this age or this time in my life. There have been so many things in my life, and perhaps in yours as well, that were designed to take us out, but God has placed it in me to tell those who have an ear to hear that YOUR JOY IS SIGNIFICANT to get through the struggle, the disappointment, and the hurt.

Revelation 12:11 And they overcame {triumphed} him by the blood of the Lamb and by the words of their testimony; they did not love their lives to death.

The Word of God finally released me by letting me know that we are empowered by the word of our testimony. My testimony, I thought, was a bleak one.

My testimony was riddled with scars and scabs that I kept picking off.

God let me know that I had to let the scars remain to show everyone what I've gone through. Before, the scars controlled me and prevented me from opening up and allowing the world to know that I was an imperfect person walking amongst imperfect people. I tried to disguise myself and let the world see a perfect person walking around with no problems, no pain, no past, but it was very difficult to walk that walk. I found myself alone all too often, even when surrounded by many people.

I allowed God to really begin the cleansing process in me around the year 2000. I say that I allowed Him because we can hold onto a thing for so long that we don't know how to let it go, and God is a gentleman who will never force himself into us.

I remember sitting with my pastor, at the time Jason L. Johnson out of Biloxi MS. It was Father's Day, and for me, Father's Day is always a struggle. Pastor Johnson recognized that I was having an emotional breakdown after his sermon. He took me by the hand and walked me around the church and told me that he was going to be my spiritual father. He treated me truly as a daughter. That experience started a significant change in my life. God dealt with me, and the dirtiness didn't feel as dirty anymore. I was able to start what I now know was finding JOY on the journey.

Those of us that have been through a battle of any kind that has left emotional or physical scars, I say to you, wear your scars openly as a badge of honor. God has brought you through, and you have the scars to prove it! Scars are representations of the healing that has taken place in your body. There is no longer an open wound, only a scar of what was. Now you and I can use those scars, that were once open and painful with bandages that had to be changed often, as door openers to tell of the goodness of the Lord to bring glory to his name for all He has done.

God is saying, "Take the bandages off." Let the world see the scars of your past so that they prevent others from having to go through some of the same situations; but more importantly, to them to let them know that they can get through them.

The enemy definitely wanted to destroy and kill me; to damage me to the degree that I would not be able to be effective for the Kingdom of God. I'm here to tell you that for God I live; I am a part of His Kingdom, and I am a Queen. I was a Queen in the making and every one of the struggles, the situations, and the circumstances that I had to go through and endure were to make me the strong person that I am today.

Part of my assignment is to stand before the crowds and the multitudes and tell them yes, I went through an embarrassing ordeal; yes, I went through a pain that I will probably never forget, but instead of letting it control me, I took control of it. I finally was able to stand up and just stare the pain in the eye; I realized that I am royalty. As royalty, I am able to dictate, declare, and demand a better life going forward.

Being a Queen (or King) is about knowing your worth, appreciating, and loving yourself. As I came into the knowledge of who I am, I wrote the following poem to encourage myself. I hope that it encourages you as well.

I AM A QUEEN

I love myself.
I know who I am, and I know my worth.
I had to make a new start
by being true to my own heart.
I dance to the beat of a different drum.
The uniqueness of me, flaws and all,
was a gift given to me by the one and the only true
living God.
I admit I make mistakes.
I can't escape or run.
The ability that I do have
is that I choose to stand tall.
No need to compete.
Authenticity is key to my forward movement.
Obtaining the strength
and the ability to love myself has been a journey
traveled physically alone.
The result being able to share unconditional
love with others
the way that God has always shown
His agape love toward me.
I am strong, determined, witty,
JOYFUL, JOYOUS AND FREE!
But most of all I am loved by the Most High God
who has always seen me as a Queen.

We are all part of the Kingdom of God, with God assignments. Once you can see clearly what that assignment is, nothing and nobody will keep you from completing it. I was assigned to ultimately ignite, impact, and invoke JOY into those who suffer from a lack of JOY, to tell women and young girls who are or have gone through abuse similar to mine, that they, too, can be free from the feelings of unworthiness, hurt, and disappointment. I am sure that they feel these things if they haven't ever dealt with what happened to them; I am also assigned to reassure them that they can have a renewal of mind, body, and soul.

To every individual who has been abused sexually, physically, or mentally, I want you to know that you are not what happened to you. You are Queens and Kings. You will survive, and as a result of that royalty that you are, you have the right to operate within the kingdom. When you truly realize that, you will then be empowered. An empowered life is a life that doesn't look back at the shame, pain, or frustration to bask in it, but to help change the lives of others and look ahead to all the beauty and value that lies ahead.

The value of a woman is not her house, clothes, makeup, or her body. There is a value that lies deep within that can never be touched by anyone, and that value is the value of JOY. Only God gives it, and no man can take it away.

When a woman gives herself to a man, she's opening up the most valuable part of herself. Not that physical part that men lust after, but that inner part that says that she is of worth and value and that she is highly desired. The sanctity of life must be preserved. But more importantly, the sanctity of sex and of a woman's body has just as much moral value. When a woman gives herself to a man, she's giving her innermost part as well as the outer.

For me, the greatest realization was an understanding that I have something of value to share with women, that the ordeal that I went through wasn't to punish or destroy me. It was to empower me to stand before women of all ages, races, and cultural backgrounds to deliver the liberating words that *you are valuable.*

My assignment is not to punish you or cause you to feel "less than" with a hard fist to beat you down, but it is to wake within you the knowing that you are worthy of your crown and to lift you up with love, to let you know that you are valuable, and you are loved. God loved me through some awful stuff; some along the way was self-inflicted. His desire is to have you open up so that you, too, can be loved, so that one set of footprints can carry you through your ordeal, pain, frustration, disappointment, and your situation.

It may seem that your situation is singular in that you're the only one having to struggle through and deal with it. I know mine was so shameful, embarrassing, and so very difficult, that I didn't think I would live through it. Looking back and knowing that this pain was caused by a person that I should have been able to trust and rely on makes it more daunting. But I am devoted, determined, and dedicated to rise despite it all.

It must be known that there are Angels among us, and that these angels protect and provide for us. When you lead with love, love bounces back; love allows you to be able to overcome and get through the most difficult of circumstances. If you find yourself downtrodden, if you find yourself betrayed, if you find yourself damaged, know that God loves you and He wants to reach out a hand to pull you through. Know that the damage that has been inflicted on you doesn't have to define you. Instead, it refines you so that the end result is that you are able to stand taller and overcome more because you've had the opportunity to go through an ordeal.

No one wants to be damaged. No one wants to go through pain. I wanted to be a princess. I wanted to have a fairytale life. I wanted Prince Charming to come home every day and pick me up, swing me around, and tell me how wonderful I was. Instead, I endured some of the most damaging, depressing, disturbing, actions a child could go through. And yet, I was able to go through it and go to another place of victory and power. That place exists for you, but only if you open up and allow yourself the chance to heal.

I know that those of you that have gone through or are going through similar situations even right now, are convinced and believe that you shouldn't share what you have been through outside of the locked doors that it occurred in. Many of you are shamed into not saying anything, others of you are scared into not saying anything, and still others are coerced to not share this secret that shouldn't be a secret, as if you asked to be entered into this secret shame that is damaging your every cell, every aspect of your being. Many secrets have to be taken to the grave, never given the voice to set you free. Give it a voice! This happened. You couldn't stop it, yet you're still standing.

Life overcomes situations. Stop feeling sorry for yourself (I can say that now; I was once there) and become stronger than the abuser. No longer hide behind the shame. No more secret places. Every chain can be broken, every self-defeating point of darkness can be defeated when you decide to no longer live on the island called denial. You will find forgiveness.

That is the end point of this whole message. Find forgiveness, forgive the abuser, forgive the accuser, forgive the ones who knew and did nothing, but more importantly, *forgive yourself.* You see, forgiveness is not for the person that did the act, although they receive the benefit of your forgiveness. No, instead, forgiveness is for you. As long as you hold onto the hate, as long as you hold onto the hurt, you will never be able to become fully free. Yes, it happened; yes, it was nasty, negative, and in no way should have happened. But the reality is that it did, and a lot of things happen that shouldn't happen.

We could write a book on what should not happen, and what should happen. The truth is that stuff happens all the time, every day. Even as this book is being written and read, stuff is happening that is not nice. We can wallow in the bile of hatred and disappointment that it did happen, or we can climb out of the nasty pit and allow the Lord to love us back to health. Many of you, like me, came from a dysfunctional Brady Bunch family. Things on TV can look so wonderful, can't they? The housekeeper keeps the house clean, the food is always on the table, the clothes are always clean, the car is always brand-new, and the house is in a nice neighborhood. Let's be honest, many of us don't live like that; in fact, most of us don't.

Most of us live in dungeons of despair that we have to climb up out of and make our own Brady Bunch. You see, having gone through that, I would never want a child of mine or anyone that I have influence over to experience that. And yet, it's happening every day. This book can't stop it from happening. But it can help those individuals that have experienced it to get past it, move on, go on, and to reach the level of royalty that they were designed for. Stop holding your head down in shame; instead, lift your head up. He said He's a lifter of the brother.

Realize that you are beautifully and wonderfully made. Look back at your past and realize that it is not your present and it is not your future. Your deliverance comes from knowing that your best is yet to come, and then nothing can stop you from reaching that best – except you.

I pray that if you have gone through anything traumatic or are experiencing something unimaginable right now, that you realize that there is hope after trauma and that you can get unstuck from the effects of trauma in your life, too. All too many of us find ourselves stuck in the past, stuck in the pain and disappointment of somebody else's actions. I was one that was stuck, stuck with thoughts of what had taken place in my life, that it was somehow my fault, that something I said or even had done caused the act of perverse invasion into my childhood life.

There are countless instances where we place ourselves in the path of pain and as a result of our bad decisions, we experience trauma and drama. More often than not, though, we are innocent victims that get caught up in situations that are out of our control. If we want to live, if we want to continue existing and thriving, we must endure.

Endurance doesn't mean acceptance. Merriam Webster defines endurance as the ability to deal with pain or suffering for a long period of time. The apostle Paul says in 2 Timothy 2:3 that you are to endure hardship as a good soldier of Jesus Christ. Know that the process of endurance is not automatic. You have to approach endurance like a disciplined athlete, a hard-working farmer, or as Paul describes it, as a soldier, and I'll say as one that's called to do multiple deployments overseas away from the comforts of home.

Paul in 2 Timothy 2:3 is encouraging Timothy to embrace hardship for the sake of the gospel. We, too, must embrace and endure those things that cause us pain so that God gets the glory from our lives. We have to endure on this journey called life in order to get through to our moment of success, our moment of victory, and our moment of normalcy. It's not normal for little girls to be molested or abused. It's not normal for women to be beaten up by stronger, more powerful men. It's not normal for a child to be sold into sex trafficking. There are a lot of things that are not normal; however, sadly they are some people's reality.

Once a person has been delivered from the horrific conditions of any kind of abuse, that person must get help to start their deliverance journey toward some sense of normalcy. Truthfully, as a witness, after something traumatic occurs in your life, I don't think anything about you can ever be fully labeled as "normal." However, I do believe that God can and will give you JOY, unspeakable JOY, a peace that surpasses all of your understanding, and His unconditional love will take you over.

If you have experienced any kind of traumatic encounter in your life, I want you to know that you have to realize that you are not your past. You are not what happened to you, you are who you choose to be.

A Daughter's Perspective...

She was damaged before delivered....
She was confused, no identity,
shattered pieces of broken heart
engulfed in the depth of a wounded soul.
Outside, she remained as gorgeous and strong
as God had intended from day one of her creation.
Those that looked upon her would never know
the bondage and the battle taking place inside of her.
Oh, the fragile broken heart that needed mending.
Only she and God knew how deeply rooted her pain
was within, but through the pain, the hurt,
and the disappointment she smiles, serves, and shows
the love of God to all she comes in contact with.
She knew that she had to be restored.
She knew that her pain was not in vain.
She knew that upon her healing, upon her
deliverance, that the lives of many could be saved.
She turned to God the Father, the Healer,
the Alpha and the Omega, and the Author and
Finisher of her faith.
She knew that in Him she would be made whole
again.
God knew she would be a willing vessel,
the one who would reach individuals like her
who had been damaged and broken,
because she had been where they were.
I have watched God bring my mother

through many things in her life.
God has delivered her from the damage of past hurts,
disappointments, and failures.
I've seen Him divinely and supernaturally
empower her physically, to move past things
that have taken others out.
God has given my mother the power to conquer
the demons of her past, present and future,
and help those who have similar battles do the same.
And this makes me proud, that God also knew
that once delivered, this WOMAN, this FRIEND, this
QUEEN, my MOTHER, would always and forever
give Him the glory for her life.

Her daughter,
Tashira B. Hester

About the Author

Joyce Hester

A.K.A. Lady Joy

Joyce Hester is a true Joy enthusiast. Joyce is affectionately known as Lady Joy. Lady Joy is a Kingdom minded individual who loves to see all of Gods people thriving towards success in their natural capacity. Lady Joy is a mother of three beautiful children, enrichment speaker, author, mentor, Joy coach and friend to many. Most know her from her internet talk show on We Rise Media Network, "Triumph Over Trials w/Lady Joy where she welcomes the testimonies of those who have gone through traumatic experiences that have caused complacency, setback, depression and postures of stagnation over their lives. To now standing in Triumphant peace, love and Joy. Lady Joy believes in and is an advocate for women's empowerment which is why she created the non-profit organization Kingdom Women Rock Outreach Ministries, in 2016, where her goal is to see women from the North, South, East and the West come together in Unity with the spirit of collaboration not competition. Lady Joy's overall mission is to help individuals walk in freedom from the limitations that they have set for themselves through their thoughts and behaviors. Lady Joy likes to spend much of her time reaching back to the generations that are coming up. She has a true servants heart. She loves, as well as connects, with the diversity she sees throughout the world, which is why she is in the practice of engaging with a minimum of five people every time she leaves her home. She is known for her jubilant personality that causes her to never meet a stranger.

DAMAGED 2 Delivered